March of America Facsimile Series

Number 34

The Redeemed Captive
Returning to Zion

John Williams

The Redeemed Captive Returning to Zion

by John Williams

ANN ARBOR

UNIVERSITY MICROFILMS, INC.

A Subsidiary of Xerox Corporation

E
87
W735

Foreword

The Redeemed Captive returning to Zion, by John Williams, a Congregational clergyman, was first published in 1707. Williams, writing with the encouragement of Cotton Mather, described a French and Indian raid on Deerfield in the Massachusetts colony which had taken place in 1704 while he was pastor there. After recounting the horrors of the raid, Williams went on to relate his and fellow townsmen's sufferings as prisoners. He intended his narrative to provide edifying examples of Christian fortitude. From his own point of view, the greatest trial came from attempts by the French to convert him and the other prisoners to Catholicism. His account reveals the intensity of feeling about the religious question and the bitterness that it caused in the Anglo-French rivalry for control of North America. Williams' book achieved considerable popularity with the English colonists during the 18th century and was reprinted numerous times. The edition reproduced here is the sixth, printed in 1795.

In the first terrible moments of the raid on Deerfield, Williams looked on helplessly while the Indians slaughtered two of his children. The raiders then put the town to the torch and compelled their prisoners to march with them, in the dead of winter, to Canada. When it became evident that Williams' wife, still weak from childbirth, could not maintain the pace, one of the Indians killed her with his hatchet. Many others in the party succumbed. Through it all, however, Williams' religious faith sustained him. Though near collapse, he finally reached the French settlement of Chambly. There, he said, the French treated him kindly.

Very quickly, he found himself a particular target of the Jesuits, who hoped to convert him to Catholicism or, failing that, to keep him from influencing the other prisoners whom they were also trying to convert. During the two and a half years of his imprisonment in Canada, Williams was transferred from Chambly to Montreal, Quebec, and Chateauviche. Regardless of where he was, however, he could not escape religious coercion from his captors. According to Williams, a superior of the priests "boasted what they would do in Europe; and that we must expect not only in Europe, but in New-England, the establishment of popery." But if the French gloried in the superiority of Catholicism, Williams was no less sure and no less outspoken in his defense of Protestantism. When the French invited him to enter their churches, saying that had they been in New England they would have visited the Protestant churches there, Williams retorted that "the case was far different, for there was nothing...as to matter or manner of worship, but what was according to the word of God, in our churches."

Appended to the narrative is the text of a sermon which Williams preached shortly after his return to Deerfield. An appendix includes material contributed by various persons showing how the town of Deerfield had suffered over the years because of French and Indian attacks. In this edition the appendix brings the story down to 1793. The *Dictionary of American Biography* provides additional information about Williams and his writings. See also R.W.G. Vail, *The Voice of the Old Frontier* (Philadelphia, 1949), pp. 34-35.

The Redeemed Captive
Returning to Zion

THE
Redeemed Captive returning to ZION :

OR,

A FAITHFUL HISTORY

OF

Remarkable Occurrences

IN THE

CAPTIVITY AND DELIVERANCE

OF

Mr. John Williams,

Minister of the Gospel in DEERFIELD ;

Who, in the Desolation which befel that Plantation, by an Incursion of
FRENCH and INDIANS, was by them carried away, with his Family
and his Neighbourhood, into CANADA.

DRAWN UP BY HIMSELF.

Annexed to which, IS A SERMON,

PREACHED BY HIM UPON HIS RETURN.

Also, AN *A P P E N D I X*,

By the Rev. Mr. WILLIAMS, *of* Springfield.

LIKEWISE, AN *A P P E N D I X*,

By the Rev. Mr. TAYLOR, *of* Deerfield.

WITH A CONCLUSION TO THE WHOLE,

By the Rev. Mr. PRINCE, *of* Boston.

The Sixth Edition.

Printed by SAMUEL HALL, No. 53, Cornhill, BOSTON.
1795.

The DEDICATION.

JOSEPH DUDLEY, Efq.

Captain-General, and Governor in Chief, in and over her Majefty's Province of the Maffachu-fetts-Bay in New-England, &c.

SIR,

IT was a fatyrical anfwer, and deeply reproach-ful to mankind, which the philofopher gave to that queftion, *What fooneft grows old ?* Replied, *Thanks.* The reproach of it would not be fo fen-fible, were there not fenfible demonftrations of the truth of it, in thofe that wear the character of the ingenuous. Such as are at firft furprifed at, and feem to have no common relifh of divine goodnefs, yet too foon lofe the impreffion : They fang God's praife, but foon forgat his works. That it fhould be thus with refpect to our bene-factors on earth, is contrary to the ingenuity of human nature ; but that our grateful refent-ments of the fignal favours of Heaven fhould

soon

foon be worn off by time, is, to the laft degree, criminal and unpardonable.

It would be unaccountable ftupidity in me, not to maintain the moft lively and awful fenfe of divine rebukes, which the holy God has feen meet, in fpotlefs fovereignty, to difpenfe to me, my family and people, in delivering us into the hands of thofe that hated us ; who led us into a ftrange land. My foul has thefe ftill in remembrance, and is humbled in me. However, God has given us plentiful occafion to fing of mercy as well as judgment. The wonders of divine mercy, which we have feen in the land of our captivity, and deliverance therefrom, cannot be forgotten without incurring the guilt of the blackeft ingratitude.

To preferve the memory of thefe, it has been thought advifeable to publifh a fhort account of fome of thofe fignal appearances of divine power and goodnefs for us ; hoping it may ferve to excite the praife, faith and hope of all that love God ; and may peculiarly ferve to cherifh a grateful fpirit, and to render the impreffions of God's mighty works indelible on my heart, and on thofe who with me have feen the wonders of the Lord, and tafted of his falvation ; that we may not fall under that heavy charge made againft Ifrael of old, Pfal. lxxviii. 11, 42. *They forgat his works, and the wonders he fhewed them : They remembered not his hand, nor the day that he delivered them from the enemy.*

And

And I cannot, Sir, but think it moſt agreeable to my duty to God, our ſupreme redeemer, to mention your Excellency's name with honour; ſince Heaven has honoured you as the prime inſtrument in returning our captivity. Sure I am, the laws of juſtice and gratitude (which are the laws of God) do challenge from us the moſt publick acknowledgments of your uncommon ſympathy with us, your children, in our bonds, expreſſed in all endearing methods of parental care and tenderneſs. All your people are cheriſhed under your wings, happy in your government, and are obliged to bleſs God for you: And among your people, thoſe who are immediately expoſed to the outrages of the enemy, have peculiarly felt refreſhment from the benign influences of your wiſe and tender conduct; and are under the moſt ſenſible engagements to acknowledge your Excellency, under God, as the breath of their noſtrils.

Your uncommon ſagacity and prudence, in contriving to looſe the bonds of your captived children; your unwearied vigour and application, in purſuing them, to work our deliverance, can never be enough praiſed. It is moſt notorious, that nothing was thought too difficult by you to effect this deſign, in that you readily ſent your own ſon, Mr. William Dudley, to undergo the hazards and hardſhips of a tedious voyage, that this affair might be tranſacted with ſucceſs; which muſt not be forgotten, as an expreſſion of your great ſolicitude and zeal to recover us from the tyranny and oppreſſion of our captivity.

I doubt

A 2

I doubt not but that the God, whom herein you have served, will remember, and glorioufly reward you ; and may Heaven long preferve you at our helm, a blefling fo neceffary for the tranquillity of this province, in this dark and tempeftuous feafon. May the beft of bleffings, from the Father of Lights, be fhowered down upon your perfon, family and government ; which fhall be the prayer of

Your Excellency's moft humble

obedient, and dutiful fervant,

JOHN WILLIAMS.

March 3, 1706,7.

REDEEMED CAPTIVE

RETURNING TO

ZION.

THE hiftory I am going to write, proves, that days of fafting and prayer, without reformation, will not avail to turn away the anger of God from a profeffing people ; and yet wit‐ neffeth, how very advantageous, gracious fupplica‐ tions are, to prepare particular chriftians, pa‐ tiently to fuffer the will of God, in very trying publick calamities. For fome of us, moved with fear, fet apart a day of prayer, to afk of God, either to fpare, and fave us from the hands of our enemies, or to prepare us to fanctify and honour him in what way foever he fhould come forth towards us. The places of fcripture from whence we were entertained, were Gen. xxxii. 10, 11. *I am not worthy of the leaft of all the mercies, and of all the truth which thou haft fhewed unto thy fer‐ vant. Deliver me, I pray thee, from the hand of my brother, from the hand of Efau : For I fear him, left he will come and fmite me, and the mother with the children.* [In the forenoon.] And Gen. xxxii. 26.

And

*And he said, let me go, for the day breaketh : And
he said, I will not let thee go, except thou bless me.*
[In the afternoon.] From which we were called
upon to spread the causes of fear, relating to our
own selves, or families, before God ; as also, how
it becomes us, with an undeniable importunity,
to be following God, with earnest prayers for his
blessing, in every condition. And it is very ob-
servable, how God ordered our prayers, in a peculiar manner, to be going up to him ; to prepare
us, with a right christian spirit, to undergo, and
endure suffering trials.

Not long after, the holy and righteous God
brought us under great trials, as to our persons
and families, which put us under a necessity of
spreading before him, in a wilderness, the distressing dangers and calamities of our relations ; yea;
that called on us, notwithstanding seeming present frowns, to resolve by his grace not to be sent
away without a blessing. Jacob, in wrestling,
has the hollow of his thigh put out of joint ;
and it is said to him, *Let me go ;* yet he is rather
animated to an heroical, christian resolution to
continue earnest for the blessing, than discouraged
from asking.

ON the twenty-ninth of February, 1703,4,
not long before break of day, the enemy came in
like a flood upon us ; our watch being unfaithful,
an evil, whose awful effects, in a surprisal of our
fort, should bespeak all watchmen to avoid, as
they would not bring the charge of blood upon
themselves. They came to my house in the beginning of the onset, and by their violent endeavours

deavours to break open doors and windows, with
axes and hatchets, awaked me out of sleep;
on which I leaped out of bed, and running toward
the door, perceived the enemy making their en-
trance into the house. I called to awaken two
soldiers, in the chamber; and returned toward
my bed-side, for my arms. The enemy immediately brake into the room, I judge to the number of twenty, with painted faces, and hideous
acclamations. I reached up my hands to the
bed-tester, for my pistol, uttering a short petition
to God, for everlasting mercies for me and mine,
on the account of the merits of our glorified Redeemer; expecting a present passage through the
valley of the shadow of death; saying in myself,
as Isaiah xxxviii. 10, 11. *I said, in the cutting off
my days, I shall go to the gates of the grave: I am
deprived of the residue of my years. I said, I shall
not see the Lord, even the Lord, in the land of the
living: I shall behold man no more with the inhabitants of the world.* Taking down my pistol, I
cocked it, and put it to the breast of the first Indian who came up; but my pistol missing fire, I
was seized by three Indians, who disarmed me,
and bound me naked, as I was in my shirt, and
so I stood for near the space of an hour. Binding
me, they told me they would carry me to Quebec. My pistol missing fire was an occasion of
my life's being preserved; since which I have
also found it profitable to be crossed in my own
will. The judgment of God did not long slum-
ber against one of the three which took me, who
was a captain, for by sun-rising he received a
mortal shot from my next neighbour's house;
                                                who

who oppofed fo great a number of French and Indians as three hundred, and yet were no more than feven men in an ungarrifoned houfe.

I cannot relate the diftreffing care I had for my dear wife, who had lain-in but a few weeks before, and for my poor children, family, and chriftian neighbours. The enemy fell to rifling the houfe, and entered in great numbers into every room of the houfe. I begged of God to remember mercy in the midft of judgment ; that he would fo far reftrain their wrath, as to prevent their murdering of us ; that we might have grace to glorify his name, whether in life or death ; and, as I was able, committed our ftate to God. The enemies who entered the houfe were all of them Indians and Macquas, infulted over me a while, holding up hatchets over my head, threatening to burn all I had ; but yet God, beyond expectation, made us in a great meafure to be pitied ; for though fome were fo cruel and barbarous as to take and carry to the door, two of my children, and murder them, as alfo a negro woman ; yet they gave me liberty to put on my clothes, keeping me bound with a cord on one arm, till I put on my clothes to the other ; and then changing my cord, they let me drefs myfelf, and then pinioned me again : Gave liberty to my dear wife to drefs herfelf, and our children. About fun an hour high, we were all carried out of the houfe, for a march; and faw many of the houfes of my neighbours in flames, perceiving the whole fort, one houfe excepted, to be taken. Who can tell what forrows pierced our fouls, when we faw ourfelves carried away from God's
fanctuary,

fanctuary, to go into a ftrange land, expofed to fo many trials ? The journey being at leaft three hundred miles we were to travel ; the fnow up to the knees, and we never inured to fuch hardfhips and fatigues ; the place we were to be carried to, a popifh country. Upon my parting from the town, they fired my houfe and barn. We were carried over the river, to the foot of the mountain, about a mile from my houfe, where we found a great number of our chriftian neighbours, men, women and children, to the number of an hundred, nineteen of whom were afterward murdered by the way, and two ftarved to death, near Cowafs, in a time of great fcarcity or famine, the favages underwent there. When we came to the foot of the mountain, they took away our fhoes, and gave us, in the room of them, Indian fhoes, to prepare us for our travel. Whilft we were there, the Englifh beat out a company, that remained in the town, and purfued them to the river, killing and wounding many of them ; but the body of the army, being alarmed, they repulfed thofe few Englifh that purfued them.

I am not able to give you an account of the number of the enemy flain ; but I obferved after this fight, no great infulting mirth, as I expected ; and faw many wounded perfons, and for feveral days together they buried of their party, and one of chief note among the Macquas. The governour of Canada told me, his army had that fuccefs with the lofs of but eleven men, three Frenchmen, one of whom was the lieutenant of the army, five Macquas, and three Indians : But after my arrival at Quebec, I fpake with an Englifhman,

lifhman, who was taken the laft war, and married there, and of their religion ; who told me, they loft above forty, and that many were wounded. I replied, the governour of Canada faid they loft but eleven men. He anfwered, it is true, that there were but eleven killed out-right at the taking of the fort, but that many others were wounded, among whom was the enfign of the French ; but, faid he, they had a fight in the meadow, and that in both engagements they loft more than forty. Some of the foldiers, both French and Indians, then prefent, told me fo, (faid he), adding, that the French always endeavour to conceal the number of their flain.

After this, we went up the mountain, and faw the fmoke of the fires in town, and beheld the awful defolations of Deerfield : And before we marched any farther, they killed a fucking child of the Englifh. There were flain by the enemy, of the inhabitants of our town, to the number of thirty-eight, befides nine of the neighbouring towns. We travelled not far the firft day ; God made the heathen fo to pity our children, that though they had feveral wounded perfons of their own to carry upon their fhoulders for thirty miles, before they came to the river, yet they carried our children, incapable of travelling, upon their fhoulders, and in their arms. When we came to our lodging place, the firft night, they dug away the fnow, and made fome wigwams, cut down fome of the fmall branches of fpruce trees to lie down on, and gave the prifoners fomewhat to eat ; but we had but little appetite. I was pinioned, and bound down that night, and fo I was
                                                            every

every night whilſt I was with the army. Some of the enemy who brought drink with them from the town, fell to drinking, and in their drunken fit they killed my negro man, the only dead perſon I either ſaw at the town, or in the way. In the night an Engliſhman made his eſcape. In the morning I was called for, and ordered by the general to tell the Engliſh, that if any more made their eſcape, they would burn the reſt of the priſoners. He that took me was unwilling to let me ſpeak with any of the priſoners, as we marched ; but on the morning of the ſecond day, he being appointed to guard the rear, I was put into the hands of my other maſter, who permitted me to ſpeak to my wife, when I overtook her, and to walk with her, to help her in her journey. On the way we diſcourſed of the happineſs of thoſe who had a right to an houſe not made with hands, eternal in the heavens ; and God for a father, and friend ; as alſo, that it was our reaſonable duty, quietly to ſubmit to the will of God, and to ſay, the will of the Lord be done. My wife told me her ſtrength of body began to fail, and that I muſt expect to part with her ; ſaying, ſhe hoped God would preſerve my life, and the life of ſome, if not of all of our children, with us ; and commended to me, under God, the care of them. She never ſpake any diſcontented word as to what had befallen us, but with ſuitable expreſſions juſtified God in what had befallen us. We ſoon made an halt, in which time my chief ſurviving maſter came up, upon which I was put upon marching with the foremoſt, and ſo made to take my laſt farewell of my dear wife,

B   the

the defire of my eyes, and companion in many mercies and afflictions. Upon our feparation from each other, we afked for each other, grace fufficient for what God fhould call us to. After our being parted from one another, fhe fpent the few remaining minutes of her ftay in reading the holy fcriptures ; which fhe was wont perfonally every day to delight her foul in reading, praying, meditating of, and over, by herfelf, in her clofet, over and above what fhe heard out of them in our family worfhip. I was made to wade over a fmall river, and fo were all the Englifh, the water above knee-deep, the ftream very fwift ; and after that, to travel up a fmall mountain ; my ftrength was almoft fpent, before I came to the top of it. No fooner had I overcome the difficulty of that afcent, but I was permitted to fit down, and be unburthened of my pack. I fat pitying thofe who were behind, and intreated my mafter to let me go down, and help up my wife ; but he refufed, and would not let me ftir from him. I afked each of the prifoners (as they paffed by me) after her, and heard that in paffing through the abovefaid river, fhe fell down, and was plunged over head and ears in the water ; after which fhe travelled not far ; for at the foot of this mountain, the cruel and blood-thirfty favage, who took her, flew her with his hatchet, at one ftroke ; the tidings of which were very awful ; and yet fuch was the hard heartednefs of the adverfary, that my tears were reckoned to me as a reproach. My lofs, and the lofs of my children, was great ; our hearts were fo filled with forrow, that nothing but the comfortable

hopes

hopes of her being taken away in mercy to herfelf, from the evils we were to fee, feel, and fuffer
under, (and joined to the affembly of the fpirits
of juft men made perfect, to reft in peace, and
joy unfpeakable, and full of glory, and the good
pleafure of God thus to exercife us), could have
kept us from finking under, at that time. That
fcripture, Job i. 21. *Naked came I out of my
mother's womb, and naked fhall I return thither;
the Lord gave, and the Lord hath taken away, bleffed
be the name of the Lord;* was brought to my mind,
and from it, that an afflicting God was to be
glorified; with fome other places of fcripture, to
perfuade to a patient bearing my afflictions.

We were again called upon to march, with a
far heavier burden on my fpirits, than on my
back. I begged of God to over-rule, in his providence, that the corpfe of one fo dear to me, and
of one whofe fpirit he had taken to dwell with
him in glory, might meet with a chriftian burial,
and not be left for meat to the fowls of the air,
and beafts of the earth : A mercy that God gra-
cioufly vouchfafed to grant : For God put it into
the hearts of my neighbours to come out as far as
fhe lay, to take up her corpfe, recarry it to the
town, and decently to bury it, foon after. In
our march they killed another fucking infant of
one of my neighbours ; and before night, a girl,
of about eleven years of age. I was made to
mourn at the confideration of my flock's being
fo far a flock of flaughter, many being flain in the
town, and fo many murdered in fo few miles from
the town ; and from fears what we muft yet expect from fuch who delightfully imbrued their
hands

hands in the blood of fo many of his people.
When we came to our lodging place, an Indian
captain from the eaftward fpake to my mafter
about killing of me, and taking off my fcalp.   I
lifted up my heart to God, to implore his grace and
mercy in fuch a time of need ; and afterwards I
told my mafter, if he intended to kill me, I defired he would let me know of it, affuring him
that my death, after a promife of quarter, would
bring the guilt of blood upon him.   He told me
he would not kill me.   We laid down and flept,
for God fuftained and kept us.   In the morning
we were all called before the chief fachems of the
Macquas and Indians, that a more equal diftri-
bution might be made of the prifoners among
them.   At my going from the wigwam, my beft
clothing was taken away from me.   As I came
nigh the place appointed, fome of the captives
met me, and told me, they thought the enemies
were going to burn fome of us, for they had peel-
ed off the bark from feveral trees, and acted very
ftrangely.   To whom I replied, they could act
nothing againft us, but as they were permitted of
God, and I was perfuaded he would prevent fuch
feverities.   When we came to the wigwam appointed, feveral of the captives were taken from
their former mafters, and put into the hands of
others : But I was fent again to my two mafters,
who brought me from my houfe.

In our fourth day's march, the enemy killed
another of my neighbours, who being near the
time of travail, was wearied with her journey.
When we came to the great river, the enemy
took fleighs to draw their wounded, feveral of
our

our children, and their packs; and marched a great pace. I travelled many hours in water up to the ankles. Near night I was very lame, having before my travel wrenched my ankle-bone and finews. I thought, fo did others, that I fhould not be able to hold out to travel far. I lifted up my heart to God (my only refuge) to remove my lamenefs, and carry me through with my children and neighbours, if he judged it beft. However, I defired God would be with me in my great change, if he called me by fuch a death to glorify him; and that he would take care of my children and neighbours, and blefs them; and within a little fpace of time, I was well of my lamenefs, to the joy of my children and neighbours, that faw fo great an alteration in my travelling.

On the Saturday, the journey was long and tedious; we travelled with fuch fpeed, that four women were tired, and then flain by them who led them captive.

On the Sabbath day we refted, and I was permitted to pray and preach to the captives. The place of fcripture fpoken from, was Lam. i. 18. *The Lord is righteous, for I have rebelled againft his commandment: Hear, I pray you, all people, and behold my forrow: My virgins and my young men are gone into captivity.* The enemy, who faid to us, fing us one of Zion's fongs, were ready, fome of them, to upbraid us, becaufe our finging was not fo loud as theirs. When the Macquas and Indians were chief in power, we had this revival in our bondage; to join together in the worfhip of God, and encourage one another to a patient

bearing

bearing the indignation of the Lord, till he should plead our caufe. When we àrrived at New-France we were forbidden praying one with another, or joining together in the fervice of God.

The next day, foon after we marched, we had an alarm ; on which many of the Englifh were bound. I was then near the front, and my maf-ters not with me ; fo I was not bound. This alarm was occafioned by fome Indians fhooting at geefe that flew over them, that put them into a confiderable confternation and fright ; but after they came to underftand they were not purfued by the Englifh, they boafted, that the Englifh would not come out after them, as they had boafted before we began our journey in the morn-ing. They killed this day two women, who were fo faint they could not travel.

The next day, in the morning, before we travelled, one Mary Brooks, a pious young wo-man, came to the wigwam where I was, and told me, fhe defired to blefs God, who had inclined the heart of her mafter to let her come to take her farewell of me. Said fhe, by my falls on the ice yefterday I injured myfelf, caufing a mifcarriage this night, fo that I am not able to travel far ; I know they will kill me to-day ; but (fays fhe) God has (praifed be his name) by his fpirit with his word, ftrengthened me to my laft encounter with death : And mentioned to me fome places of fcripture feafonably fent in for her fupport. And (fays fhe) I am not afraid of death ; I can, through the grace of God, chearfully fubmit to the will of God. Pray for me (faid fhe) at parting,

ing, that God would take me to himfelf. Accordingly fhe was killed that day. I mention it
to the end, I may ftir up all in their young days,
to improve the death of Chrift by faith, to a
giving them an holy boldnefs in the day of death.

The next day we were made to fcatter one
from another into fmaller companies ; and one of
my children carried away with Indians belonging
to the eaftern parts. At night my mafter came
to me, with my piftol in his hand, and put it to
my breaft, and faid, now I will kill you, for (faid
he) at your houfe you would have killed me with
it if you could. But, by the grace of God, I was
not much daunted ; and whatever his intention
might be, God prevented my death.

The next day I was again permitted to pray
with that company of captives with me, and we
allowed to fing a pfalm together. After which,
I was taken from all the company of the Englifh,
excepting two children of my neighbours, one of
which, a girl of four years of age, was killed by
her Macqua mafter, the next morning, the fnow
being fo deep, when we left the river, that he
could not carry the child and his pack too.

When the Sabbath came, one Indian ftaid with
me, and a little boy nine years old, whilft the
reft went a hunting. And when I was here, I
thought with myfelf, that God had now feparated
me from the congregation of his people, who
were now in his fanctuary, where he command-
eth the bleffing, even life forever ; and made to
bewail my unfruitfulnefs under, and unthankful-
nefs for fuch a mercy. When my fpirit was almoft overwhelmed within me, at the confideration

tion of what had passed over me, and what was to be expected, I was ready almost to sink in my spirit. But God spake those words with a greater efficacy than man could speak them, for my strengthening and support: Psal. cxviii. 17. *I shall not die, but live : And declare the works of the Lord.* Psalm xlii. 11. *Why art thou cast down, O my soul ? And why art thou disquieted within me ? Hope thou in God ; for I shall yet praise him, who is the health of my countenance, and my God.* Nehem. i. 8, 9. *Remember, I beseech thee, the word that thou commandest thy servant Moses, saying, if ye transgress, I will scatter you abroad among the nations : But if ye turn unto me, and keep my commandments, and do them ; though there were of you cast out unto the uttermost part of the heaven, yet will I gather them from thence, and will bring them unto the place that I have chosen, to set my name there.* These three places of scripture, one after another, by the grace of God, strengthened my hopes, that God would so far restrain the wrath of the adversary, that the greatest number of us left alive, should be carried through so tedious a journey : That though my children had no father to take care of them, that word quieted me to a patient waiting to see the end the Lord would make, Jer. xlix. 11. *Leave thy fatherless children, I will preserve them alive, and let thy widows trust in me.* Accordingly God carried them wonderfully through great difficulties and dangers. My youngest daughter, aged seven years, was carried all the journey, and looked after with a great deal of tenderness. My youngest son, aged four years, was wonderfully preserved from death ; for though they that carried

ried him, or drawed him on fleighs, were tired
with their journey, yet their favage cruel tempers
were fo over-ruled by God, that they did not kill
him; but in their pity, he was fpared, and others
would take care of him; fo that four times on
the journey he was thus preferved, till at laft he
arrived at Montreal, where a French gentlewoman, pitying the child, redeemed it out of the
hands of the heathen. My fon Samuel, and my
eldeft daughter, were pitied, fo as to be drawn
on fleighs, when unable to travel. And though
they fuffered very much through fcarcity of
food, and tedious journeys, they were carried
through to Montreal. And my fon Stephen,
about eleven years of age, wonderfully preferved
from death, in the famine whereof three Englifh
perfons died, and after eight months brought
into Chamblee.

My mafter returned on the evening of the Sabbath, and told me, he had killed five moofe.
The next day we removed to the place where he
had killed them. We tarried there three days,
till we had roafted and dried the meat. My
mafter made me a pair of fnow-fhoes, for (faid
he) you cannot poffibly travel without, the fnow
being knee-deep. We parted from thence heavy
laden; I travelled with a burden on my back,
with fnow-fhoes, twenty-five miles the firft day
of wearing them; and again the next day till afternoon; and then we came to the French river.
My mafter, at this place, took away my pack,
and drawed the whole load on the ice; but my
bones feemed to be mifplaced, and I unable to
travel with any fpeed. My feet were very fore,
                                                    and

and each night I wrung blood out of my ſtock-
ings, when I pulled them off.   My ſhins alſo
were very ſore, being cut with cruſty ſnow, in the
time of my travelling without ſnow-ſhoes.   But
finding ſome dry oak-leaves, by the river banks,
I put them to my ſhins ; and in once applying of
them, they were healed.   And here my maſter
was very kind to me, would always give me the
beſt he had to eat ; and by the goodneſs of God,
I never wanted a meal's meat, during my captivity ; though ſome of my children and neighbours were greatly wounded, (as I may ſay) with
the arrows of famine and pinching want ; having
for many days nothing but roots to live upon,
and not much of them neither.   My maſter gave
me a piece of a bible ; never diſturbed me in
reading the ſcriptures, or in praying to God.
Many of my neighbours, alſo, found that mercy
in their journey, to have bibles, pſalm books,
catechiſms, and good books, put into their hands,
with liberty to uſe them ; and yet after their arrival at Canada, all poſſible endeavours were uſed
to deprive them of them.   Some of them ſay,
their bibles were demanded by the French prieſts,
and never re-delivered to them, to their great
grief and ſorrow.

My march on the French river was very ſore ;
for fearing a thaw, we travelled a very great
pace ; my feet were ſo bruiſed, and my joints ſo
diſtorted by my travelling in ſnow ſhoes, that I
thought it impoſſible to hold out.   One morning, a little before break of day, my maſter came
and awaked me out of my ſleep, ſaying, ariſe,
pray to God, and eat your breakfaſt, for we muſt

go

go a great way to-day. After prayer, I arose from my knees, but my feet were so tender, swoln, bruised, and full of pain, that I could scarce stand upon them, without holding on the the wigwam. And when the Indians said, you must run to-day; I answered, I could not run : My master pointing out to his hatchet, said to me, then I must dash out your brains, and take off your scalp. I said, I suppose then you will do so, for I am not able to travel with speed. He sent me away alone, on the ice. About sun half an hour high, he over-took me, for I had gone very slowly, not thinking it possible to travel five miles. When he came up, he called me to run ; I told him I could go no faster. He passed by without saying one word more ; so that some-times I scarce saw any thing of him for an hour together. I travelled from about break of day till dark ; never so much as set down at noon to eat warm victuals ; eating frozen meat, which I had in my coat pocket, as I travelled. We went that day two of their day's journey, as they came down. I judge we went forty or forty-five miles that day. God wonderfully supported me ; and so far renewed my strength, that in the afternoon I was stronger to travel than in the forenoon. My strength was restored and renewed to admiration. We should never distrust the care and compassion of God, who can give strength to them who have no might, and power to them who are ready to faint.

When we entered on the lake, the ice was very rough and uneven, which was very grievous to my feet, that could scarce endure to be set down

on

on the fmooth ice, on the river. I lifted up my cry to God in ejaculatory requefts, that he would take notice of my ftate, and fome way or other relieve me. I had not marched above half a mile, before there fell a moift fnow, about an inch and half deep, that made it very foft for my feet, to pafs over the lake, to the place where my mafter's family was. Wonderful favours in the midft of trying afflictions! We went a day's journey from the lake, to a fmall company of Indians, who were a hunting; they were, after their manner, kind to me, and gave me the beft they had, which was moofe-flefh, ground-nuts, and cramberries, but no bread. For three weeks together I eat no bread. After our ftay there, and undergoing difficulties in cutting of wood, and fuffering from loufinefs, having loufy old clothes of foldiers put upon me, when they ftript me of mine, to fell to the French foldiers in the army.

We again began a march for Chamblee; we ftayed at a branch of the lake, and feafted two or three days on geefe we killed there. After another day's travel, we came to a river where the ice was thawed; we made a canoe of elm-bark in one day, and arrived on a Saturday near noon, at Chamblee, a fmall village, where is a garrifon and fort of French foldiers.

[*At* CHAMBLEE.]

This village is about fifteen miles from Mont-real. The French were very kind to me. A gentleman of the place took me into his houfe, and to his table; and lodged me at night on a good feather-bed. The inhabitants and officers were very obliging to me, the little time I ftaid

with

with them, and promifed to write a letter to the
governor in chief, to inform him of my paffing
down the river.   Here I faw a girl taken from our
town, and a young man, who informed me, that
the greateft part of the captives were come in,
and that two of my children were at Montreal ;
that many of the captives had been in three
weeks before my arrival.   Mercy in the midft of
judgment ! As we paffed along the river towards
Sorel, we went into a houfe, where was an
Englifh woman of our town, who had been left
among the French in order to her conveyance to
the Indian fort.   The French were very kind to
her, and to myfelf, and gave us the beft provifion
they had ; and fhe embarked with us, to go down
to St. François fort.   When we came down to
the firft inhabited houfe at Sorel, a French woman came to the river fide, and defired us to go
into her houfe ; and when we were entered, fhe
compaffioned our ftate, and told us, fhe had in
the laft war been a captive among the Indians,
and therefore was not a little fenfible of our
difficulties.   She gave the Indians fomething to
eat in the chimney corner, and fpread a cloth on
the table for us with napkins ; which gave fuch
offence to the Indians, that they hafted away,
and would not call in at the fort. But where-
ever we entered into houfes, the French were
very courteous.   When we came to St. François
river, we found fome difficulty by reafon of the
ice ; and entering into a Frenchman's houfe, he
gave us a loaf of bread, and fome fifh to carry
away with us ; but we paffed down the river till
night, and there feven of us fupped on the fifh
C   called

called bull-head or pout, and did not eat it up, the fish was so very large.

The next morning we met with such a great quantity of ice, that we were forced to leave our canoe, and travel on land. We went to a French officer's house, who took us into a private room, out of the fight of the Indians, and treated us very courteously. That night we arrived at the fort called St. François ; where we found several poor children, who had been taken from the eastward the summer before ; a fight very affecting, they being in habit very much like Indians, and in manners very much symbolizing with them. At this fort lived two jesuits, one of which was made superiour of the jesuits at Quebec. One of these jesuits met me at the fort gate, and asked me to go into the church, and give God thanks for preserving my life. I told him I would do that in some other place. When the bell rang for evening prayers, he that took me, bid me go ; but I refused. The jesuit came to our wigwam, and prayed a short prayer, and invited me to sup with them, and justified the Indians in what they did against us ; rehearsing some things done by major Walden, above thirty years ago ; and how justly God retaliated them in the last war, and inveighed against us for beginning this war with the Indians : And said, we had before the last winter, and in the winter, been very barbarous and cruel, in burning and killing Indians. I told them, that the Indians, in a very perfidious manner, had committed murders on many of our inhabitants, after the signing articles of peace : And as to what they spake of cruelties, they

they were undoubtedly falfehoods, for I well knew
the Englifh were not approvers of any inhuman-
ity or barbarity towards enemies.   They faid, an
Englifhman had killed one of St. Cafteen's relations, which occafioned this war ; for, fay they,
the nations, in a general counfel, had concluded
not to engage in the war, on any fide, till they
themfelves were firft molefted, and then all of
them, as one, would engage againft them that
began a war with them ; and that upon the killing of Cafteen's kinfman, a poft was difpatched
to Canada, to advertife the Macquas, and Indians,
that the Englifh had begun a war : On which
they gathered up their forces, and that the French
joined with them, to come down on the eaftern
parts ; and that when they came near New-
England, feveral of the eaftern Indians told them
of the peace made with the Englifh, and the
fatisfaction given them from the Englifh for that
murder.   But the Macquas told them, it was
now too late ; for they were fent for, and were
now come, and would fall on them, if without
their confent they made a peace with the Englifh.
Said alfo that a letter was fhown them, fent from
the governour of Port-Royal, which, he faid, was
taken in an Englifh fhip, being a letter from the
queen of England to our governour, writing how
fhe approved his defigns to enfnare and deceit-
fully to feize on the Indians ; fo that being enraged from that letter, and being forced, as it
were, they began the prefent war.   I told them
the letter was a lie, forged by the French.

The next morning the bell rang for mafs : My
mafter bid me go to church : I refufed : He
threatened

threatened me, and went away in a rage. At noon, the jefuits fent for me to dine with them ; for I eat at their table all the time I was at the fort. And after dinner, they told me, the Indians would not allow of any of their captives ftaying in their wigwams, whilft they were at church ; and were refolved by force and violence to bring us all to church, if we would not go without. I told them it was highly unreafonable fo to impofe upon thofe who were of a contrary religion ; and to force us to be prefent at fuch fervice, as we abhorred, was nothing becoming chriftianity. They replied, they were favages, and would not hearken to reafon, but would have their wills : Said alfo, if they were in New-England themfelves, they would go into their churches, to fee their ways of worfhip. I anfwered, the cafe was far different, for there was nothing (themfelves being judges) as to matter or manner of worfhip, but what was according to the word of God, in our churches ; and therefore it could not be an offence to any man's confcience. But among them, there were idolatrous fuperftitions in worfhip. They faid, Come and fee, and offer us conviction of what is fuperftitious in worfhip. To which I anfwered, That I was not to do evil that good might come on it ; and that forcing in matters of religion was hateful. They anfwered, The Indians were refolved to have it fo, and they could not pacify them without my coming ; and they would engage they fhould offer no force or violence to caufe any compliance with their ceremonies.

The next mafs, my mafter bid me go to church :

church : I objected ; he arose, and forcibly pulled me by my head and shoulders out of the wigwam to the church, which was near the door.
So I went in, and sat down behind the door ;
and there saw a great confusion, instead of any
gospel order ; for one of the jesuits was at
the altar, saying mass in a tongue unknown to
the savages ; and the other, between the altar
and the door, saying and singing prayers among
the Indians at the same time ; and many others
were at the same time saying over their pater
nosters, and Ave Mary, by tale from their chapelit,
or beads on a string. At our going out, we smil-
ed at their devotion so managed ; which was of-
fensive to them ; for they said we made a derision
of their worship. When I was here, a certain
savagess died ; one of the jesuits told me she was
a very holy woman, who had not committed one
sin in twelve years. After a day or two, the
jesuits asked me what I thought of their way, now
I saw it ? I told them, I thought Christ said of
it, as Mark vii. 7, 8, 9. *Howbeit, in vain do they
worship me, teaching for doctrines the commandments
of men. For laying aside the commandment of God,
ye hold the tradition of men, as the washing of pots
and cups ; and many other such like things ye do.
And he said unto them, Full well ye reject the commandment of God, that ye may keep your own tradition.* They told me, they were not the commandments of men, but apostolical traditions, of
equal authority with the holy scriptures : And
that after my death, I should bewail my not praying to the Virgin Mary ; and that I should find
the want of her intercession for me with her son ;

C 2   judging

judging me to hell for afferting the fcriptures to be a perfect rule of faith : And faid, I abounded in my own fenfe, entertaining explications contrary to the fenfe of the pope, regularly fitting with a general council, explaining fcripture, and making articles of faith. I told them, it was my comfort that Chrift was to be my judge, and not they, at the great day ; and as for their cenfuring and judging me, I was not moved with it.

One day, a certain favagefs, taken prifoner in Philip's war, who had lived at Mr. Buckley's at Weathersfield, called Ruth, who could fpeak Englifh very well, who had been often at my houfe, but was now profelyted to the Romifh faith, came into the wigwam, and with her an Englifh maid, who was taken the laft war, who was dreffed up in Indian apparel, unable to fpeak one word of Englifh, who faid fhe could neither tell her own name, or the name of the place from whence fhe was taken. Thefe two talked in the Indian dialect with my mafter a long time ; after which, my mafter bade me crofs myfelf ; I told him I would not ; he commanded me feveral times, and I as often refufed. Ruth faid, Mr. Williams, you know the fcripture, and therefore act againft your own light ; for you know the fcripture faith, *fervants obey your mafters ;* he is your mafter, and you his fervant. I told her fhe was ignorant, and knew not the meaning of the fcripture, telling her, I was not to difobey the great God to obey any mafter, and that I was ready to fuffer for God, if called thereto : On which fhe talked to my mafter ; I fuppofe fhe interpreted what I faid. My mafter took hold
of

of my hand to force me to crofs myfelf ; but I
ftruggled with him, and would not fuffer him to
guide my hand ; upon this, he pulled off a crucifix from his own neck, and bade me kifs it ;
but I refufed once and again ; he told me he
would dafh out my brains with his hatchet if I
refufed. I told him I fhould fooner choofe death
than to fin againft God. Then he ran and
catched up his hatchet, and acted as though he
would have- dafhed out my brains. Seeing I
was not moved, he threw down his hatchet, faying he would firft bite off all my nails if I ftill
refufed. I gave him my hand, and told him I
was ready to fuffer ; he fet his teeth in my thumb
nail, and gave a gripe with his teeth, and then
faid, *no good minifter, no love God, as bad as the devil ;*
and fo left off. I have reafon to blefs God, who
ftrengthened me to withftand. By this he was fo
difcouraged as never more to meddle with me
about my religion. I afked leave of the jefuits
to pray with thofe Englifh of our town who were
with me ; but they abfolutely refufed to give us
any permiffion to pray one with another, and did
what they could to prevent our having any difcourfe together.

After a few days, the governour de Vaudreuil,
governour in chief, fent down two men with
letters to the jefuits, defiring them to order my
being fent up to him to Montreal ; upon which,
one of the jefuits went with my two mafters, and
took me along with them, as alfo two more of
Deerfield, a man, and his daughter about feven
years of age. When we came to the lake, the
wind was tempeftuous, and contrary to us, fo
                                                    that

that they were afraid to go over ; they landed, and kindled a fire, and said they would wait a while to see whether the wind would fall or change. I went aside from the company, among the trees, and spread our case, with the temptations of it, before God, and pleaded that he would order the season so, that we might not go back again, but be furthered on our voyage, that I might have opportunity to see my children and neighbours, and converse with them, and know their state. When I returned, the wind was more boisterous ; and then a second time, and the wind was more fierce. I reflected upon myself for my unquietness, and the want of a resigned will to the will of God. And a third time went and bewailed before God my anxious cares, and the tumultuous workings of my own heart, begged a will fully resigned to the will of God, and thought that by the grace of God I was brought to say *amen* to whatever God should determine. Upon my return to the company, the wind was yet high : The jesuit and my master said, Come, we will go back again to the fort, for there is no likelihood of proceeding in our voyage, for very frequently such a wind continues three days, sometimes six. After it continued so many hours, I said to them, The will of the Lord be done ; and the canoe was put again into the river, and we embarked. No sooner had my master put me into the canoe, and put off from the shore, but the wind fell ; and coming into the middle of the river, they said, We may go over the lake well enough : And so we did. I promised, if God gave me opportunity, I would stir up others to glorify God in a

continued

continued perfevering, committing their ftraits of heart to him. He is a prayer-hearing God, and the ftormy winds obey him. After we paffed over the lake, the French, wherever we came, were very compaffionate to us.

[*At* MONTREAL.]

When I came to Montreal, which was eight weeks after my captivity, the governour de Vaudreuil redeemed me out of the hands of the Indians, gave me good clothing, took me to his table, gave me the ufe of a very good chamber, and was in all refpects, relating to my outward man, courteous and charitable to admiration. At my firft entering into his houfe, he fent for my two children, who were in the city, that I might fee them ; and promifed to do what he could to get all my children and neighbours out of the hands of the favages. My change of diet, after the difficulties of my journeys, caufed an alteration in my body : I was phyficked, blooded, and very tenderly taken care of in my ficknefs. The governour redeemed my eldeft daughter out of the hands of the Indians ; and fhe was carefully tended in the hofpital, until fhe was well of her lamenefs ; and by the governour provided for with refpect, during her ftay in the country. My youngeft child was redeemed by a gentlewoman in the city, as the Indians paffed by. After the Indians had been at their fort, and difcourfed with the priefts, they came back, and offered to the gentlewoman a man for the child, alleging that the child could not be profitable to her, but the man would, for he was a weaver, and his fervice would much advance the defign fhe had of making

ing cloth : But God over-ruled so far, that this temptation to the woman prevailed not for an exchange ; for had the child gone to the Indian fort, in an ordinary way it had abode there still, as the rest of the children carried thither do. The governour gave orders to certain officers to get the rest of my children out of the hands of the Indians, and as many of my neighbours as they could. After six weeks, a merchant of the city obtained my eldest son, who was taken to live with him. He took a great deal of pains to persuade the savages to part with him. An Indian came to the city (Sagamore George of Pennicook) from Cowass, and brought word of my son Stephen's being near Cowass, and some money was put into his hand for his redemption, and a promise of full satisfaction if he brought him ; but the Indian proved unfaithful, and I never saw my child till a year after.

The governour ordered a priest to go along with me to see my youngest daughter among the Macquas, and endeavour for her ransom. I went with him ; he was very courteous to me ; and from his parish, which was near the Macqua fort, he wrote a letter to the jesuit, to desire him to send my child to see me, and to speak with them who took her, to come along with her. But the jesuit wrote back a letter, That I should not be permitted to speak with, or see my child ; and if I came, my labour would be lost ; and that the Macquas would as soon part with their hearts as my child. At my return to the city, I with an heavy heart carried the jesuit's letter to the governour, who, when he read it, was very angry, and

and endeavoured to comfort me, affuring me I
fhould fee her, and fpeak with her ; and he would
to his utmoft endeavour for her ranfom. Accordingly, he fent to the jefuits, who were in
the city, and bid them improve their intereft for
the obtaining the child. After fome days, he
went with me in his own perfon to the fort.
When we came thither, he difcourfed with the
jefuits ; after which, my child was brought into
the chamber where I was. I was told I might
fpeak with her, but fhould be permitted to fpeak
to no other Englifh perfon there. My child was
about feven years old ; I difcourfed with her
near an hour ; fhe could read very well, and had
not forgotten her catechifm ; and was very de-
firous to be redeemed out of the hands of the Macquas, and bemoaned her ftate among them, telling me how they profaned God's Sabbaths ;
and faid, fhe thought that a few days before they
had been mocking the devil, and that one of the
jefuits ftood and looked on them. I told her,
fhe muft pray to God for his grace every day.
She faid, fhe did as fhe was able, and God helped
her ; but, fays fhe, They force me to fay fome
prayers in latin, but I do not underftand one word
of them ; I hope it will not do me any harm.
I told her, fhe muft be careful fhe did not forget
her catechifm, and the fcriptures fhe had learnt
by heart. She told the captives after I was gone,
as fome of them have fince informed me, almoft
every thing I fpake to her; and faid, fhe was
much afraid fhe fhould forget her catechifm,
having none to inftruct her. I faw her once, a
few days after, in the city, but had not many
minutes

minutes of time with her ; but what time I had, I improved to give her the best advice I could. The governour laboured much for her redemption ; at last he had a promise of it, in case he would procure for them an Indian girl in her stead. Accordingly, he sent up the river, some hundreds of leagues, for one ; but it was refused, when offered by the governour. He offered them an hundred pieces of eight for her redemption, but it was refused. His lady went over to beg her from them, but all in vain ; she is there still ; and has forgotten to speak English. Oh ! that all who peruse this history would join in their fervent requests to God, with whom all things are possible, that this poor child, and so many others of our children who have been cast upon God from the womb, and are now outcasts ready to perish, might be gathered from their dispersions, and receive sanctifying grace from God !

When I had discoursed with the child, and was coming out of the fort, one of the jesuits went out of the chamber with me, and some soldiers, to convey me to the canoe. I saw some of my poor neighbours, who stood with longing expectations to see me, and speak with me, and had leave from their savage masters so to do. I was by the jesuit himself thrust along by force, and permitted only to tell them some of their relations (they asked after) were well in the city, and that with a very audible voice ; being not permitted to come near to them. After my return to the city I was very melancholly, for I could not be permitted so much as to pray with the English,

who

who dwelt in the same house. And the English, who came to see me, were most of them put back by the guard at the door, and not suffered to come and speak with me. Sometimes the guard was so strict that I could scarce go aside on necessary occasions without a repulse; and whenever I went out into the city (a favour the governour himself never refused when I asked it of him) there were spies to watch me, and to observe whether I spake to the English. Upon which I told some of the English, they must be careful to call to mind and improve former instructions, and endeavour to stand at a further distance for a while, hoping that after a short time I should have more liberty of conversing with them. But some spies, sent out, found on a Sabbath day more than three (the number we, by their order published, were not to exceed together) of us in company, who informed the priest; the next day one of the priests told me, I had a greater number of the English with me, and that I had spoken something reflecting on their religion. I spake to the governour, desiring that no forcible means might be used with any of the captives respecting their religion; he told me, he allowed no such thing. I am persuaded that the governour, if he might act himself, would not have suffered such things to be done as have been done, and that he never did know of several things acted against the English.

At my first coming to Montreal, the governour told me, I should be sent home as soon as captain Battiss was returned, and not before; and that I was taken in order to his redemption.

D The

The governour fought by all means to divert me from my melancholy forrows, and always fhewed a willingnefs for feeing my children. And one day I told him of my defign of walking into the city ; he pleafantly anfwered, Go with all my heart. His eldeft fon went with me as far as the door, and faw the guard ftop me ; he went in and informed his father, who came to the door and afked, why they affronted the gentleman going out ? They faid, it was their order : But with an angry countenance he faid, his orders were that I fhould not be ftopt. But within a little time I had my orders to go down to Quebec. Another thing fhowing that many things are done without the governour's confent, though his name be ufed to juftify them, (viz.) I afked the prieft, after I had been at Montreal two days, leave to go and fee my youngeft child ; he faid, Whenever you would fee him, tell me, and I will bring him to you ; for, fays he, the governour is not willing you fhould go thither. And yet, not many days after, when we were at dinner, the governour's lady (feeing me fad) fpake to an officer at table, who could fpeak latin, to tell me, that after dinner I fhould go along with them and fee my two children. And accordingly after dinner I was carried to fee them ; and when I came to the houfe, I found three or four Englifh captives, who lived there, and I had leave to difcourfe with them. And not long after, the governour's lady afked me to go along with her to the hofpital, to fee one of my neighbours fick there.

One day one of the jefuits came to the governour,

our, and told the company there, that he never
faw fuch perfons as were taken from Deerfield.
Said he, The Macquas will not fuffer any of their
prifoners to abide in their wigwams whilft they
themfelves are at mafs, but carry them with them
to the church, and they cannot be prevailed with
to fall down on their knees to pray there ; but
no fooner are they returned to their wigwams,
but they fall down on their knees to prayer. He
faid, they could do nothing with the grown perfons there ; and they hindred the children's com-
plying. Whereupon, the jefuits counfelled the
Macquas to fell all the grown perfons from the
fort ; a ftratagem to feduce poor children. Oh
Lord ! Turn the counfels of thefe Ahitophels into foolifhnefs, and make the counfels of the
heathen of none effect !

Here I obferved, they were wonderfully lifted
up with pride, after the return of captain Mon-
tinug from Northampton, with news of fuccefs :
They boafted of their fuccefs againft New-England.   And they fent out an army, as they faid,
of feven hundred men, if I miftake not, two
hundred of whom were French, in company of
which army went feveral jefuits ; and faid, they
would lay defolate all the places on Connecticut
river.   The fuperiour of the priefts told me, their
general was a very prudent and brave commander, of undaunted courage, and doubted not
but they fhould have great fuccefs.   This army
went away in fuch a boafting, triumphant manner, that I had great hopes God would difcover
and difappoint their defigns ; our prayers were
not wanting for the blafting fuch a bloody defign.

fign. The fuperior of the priefts faid to me, do not flatter yourfelves in hopes of a fhort captivity ; for, faid he, there are two young princes contending for the kingdom of Spain ; and a third, that care was to be taken for his eftablifh-ment on the Englifh throne. And boafted what they would do in Europe ; and that we muft ex-pect not only in Europe, but in New-England, the eftablifhment of popery. I faid, Glory not, God can make great changes in a little time, and revive his own intereft, and yet fave his poor afflicted people. Said he, The time for miracles is vaft ; and in the time of the laft war, the king of France was, as it were, againft all the world, and yet did very great things ; but now the kingdom of Spain is for him, and the duke of Bavaria, and the duke of Savoy, &c. and fpake in a lofty manner of great things to be done by them ; and having the world, as I may fay, in fubjection to them.

I was fent down to Quebec in company of governour de Ramfey, governour of Montreal, and the fuperior of the jefuits, and ordered to live with one of the council ; from whom I received many favours for feven weeks. He told me, it was the priefts' doings to fend me down before the governour came down ; and that if I went much to fee the Englifh, or they came much to vifit me, I fhould yet certainly be fent away, where I fhould have no converfe with the Englifh.

[*At* Quebec.]

After my coming down to Quebec, I was in-vited to dine with the jefuits, and to my face they were civil enough. But after a few days, a young

gentleman

gentleman came to my chamber, and told me, that one of the jesuits (after we had done dinner) made a few distichs of verses, and gave them to his scholars to translate into French : He shewed them to me. The import of them was, " That " the king of France's grand-son had sent out his " huntsmen, and that they had taken a wolf, " who was shut up, and now he hopes the sheep " would be in safety." I knew, at the reading of them, what he aimed at ; but held my peace, as though I had been ignorant of the jesuit's intention. Observing this reproaching spirit, I said in my heart, If God will bless, let men curse if they please : And I looked to God in Christ, the great shepherd, to keep his scattered sheep among so many Romish ravenous wolves, and to remember the reproaches wherewith his holy name, ordinances, and servants were daily reproached. And upon an observation of the time of these verses being composed, I find that near the same time the bishop of Canada, with twenty ecclesiasticks, were taken by the English, as they were coming from France, and carried into England as prisoners of war.

One Sabbath day morning, I observed many signs of approaching rain, a great moisture on the stones of the hearth and chimney jambs. I was that day invited to dine with the jesuits ; and when I went up to dinner it began to rain a small drizzling rain : The superior told me, they had been praying for rain that morning : And lo, (says he), it begins to rain. I told him, I could tell him of many instances of God's hearing our prayers for rain. However, in the afternoon

there

there was a general proceſſion of all orders, prieſts, jeſuits and friars, and the citizens, in great pomp, carrying (as they ſaid) as an holy relick, one of the bones of St. Paul. The next day I was invited to the prieſts' ſeminary to dinner ; Oh, ſaid they, we went in proceſſion yeſterday for rain, and ſee what a plentiful rain followed. I anſwered, We had been anſwered when praying for rain, when no ſuch ſigns of rain, and the beginnings of rain preceeded, as now with them, before they appointed or began their proceſſion, &c. However, they upbraided me, that God did not approve of our religion, in that he diſregarded our prayers, and accepted theirs. For (ſaid they) we heard you had days of faſting and prayer before the fleet came to Quebec ; God would not regard your prayers, but heard ours, and almoſt in a miraculous way preſerved us when aſſaulted, and refuſed to hear your faſt-day prayers for your preſervation, but heard ours for your deſolation, and our ſucceſs. They boaſted alſo of their king, and his greatneſs, and ſpake of him as though there could be no ſettlement in the world but as he pleaſed ; reviling us as in a low and languiſhing caſe, having no king, but being under the government of a Queen : And ſpake as though the duke of Bavaria would in a ſhort time be emperour. From this day forward God gave them to hear ſorrowful tidings from Europe : That a war was commenced againſt the duke of Savoy, and ſo their enemies increaſed : Their biſhop taken, and two millions of wealth with him. News every year more diſtreſſing and impoveriſhing to them ; and the duke of Bavaria,

ſo

fo far from being emperour, that he is difpoffeff-
ed of his dukedom ; and France, fo far from being ftrengthened by Spain, that the kingdom of
Spain was like to be an occafion of the weaken-
ing and impoverifhing their own kingdom ; they
themfelves fo reporting. And their great army
going againft New-England turned back afham-
ed ; and they difcouraged and difheartened ; and
every year, very exercifing fears and cares, as to
the favages who live up the river. Before the
return of that army, they told me, We were led
up and down, and fold by the heathen, as fheep
for the flaughter, and they could not devife what
they fhould do with us, we fhould be fo many
prifoners, when the army returned. The jefuits
told me, it was a great mercy that fo many of our
children were brought to them, and that now,
efpecially fince they were not like fpeedily to be
returned, there was hope of their being brought
over to the Romifh faith. They would take the
Englifh children, born among them, and againft
the confent of their parents, baptize them. One
jefuit came to me and afked, whether all the
Englifh at Loret, (a place not far from Quebec,
where the favages lived), were baptized ? I told
him they were. He faid, if they be not, let me
know of it, that I may baptize them, for fear
they fhould die and be damned, if they died
without baptifm. Says he, When the favages
went againft you, I charged them to baptize all
children before they killed them ; fuch was my
defire of your eternal falvation, though you were
our enemies. There was a gentleman called
Monfieur de Beauville, a captain, the brother of
the

the lord intendant, who was a good friend to me; and very courteous to all the captives; he lent me an English bible, and when he went to France, gave it me.

All means were used to seduce poor souls.

I was invited one day to dine with one of chief note; as I was going, I met with the superiour of the jesuits coming out of the house, and he came in after dinner; and presently it was propounded to me, if I would stay among them, and be of their religion, I should have a great and honourable pension from the king every year. The superior of the jesuits turned to me, and said, ' Sir, ' you have manifested much grief and sorrow for ' your separation from so many of your neighbours ' and children; if you will now comply with this ' offer and proposal, you may have all your child- ' ren with you; and here will be enough for an ' honourable maintenance for you and them.' I answered, Sir, if I thought your religion to be true, I would embrace it freely without any such offer; but so long as I believe it to be what it is, the offer of the whole world is of no more value to me than a blackberry; and manifested such an abhorrence of this proposal, that I speedily went to take my leave and be gone. Oh! Sir (said he) sit down, why in such a hurry, you are alone in your chamber, divert yourself a little longer; and fell to other discourse; and within half an hour says again, Sir, I have one thing earnestly to re- quest of you, I pray pleasure me! I said, let your lordship speak; said he, I pray come down to the palace to-morrow morning, and honour me with your company in my coach to the great

church,

church, it being then a faints day. I anfwered,
Afk me any thing wherein I can ferve you with
a good confcience, and I am ready to gratify you,
but I muft afk your excufe here ; and immediately went away from him. Returning unto
my chamber, I gave God thanks for his upholding
of me ; and alfo made an inquiry with myfelf,
whether I had, by any action, given encouragement for fuch a temptation.

[*At* Chateauviche.]

Not many days after, and a few days before
governour de Vaudreuil's coming down, I was
fent away, fifteen miles down the river, that I
might not have opportunity of converfe with the
Englifh. I was courteoufly treated by the French,
and the prieft of that parifh ; they told me he
was one of the moft learned men in the country ;
he was a very ingenious man, zealous in their
way, but yet very familiar. I had many difputes
with the priefts who came thither ; and when
I ufed their own authors to confute fome of their
pofitions, my books, borrowed of them, were
taken away from me, for they faid, I made an ill
ufe of them. They having, many of them,
boafted of their unity in doctrine and profeffion,
were loth I fhould fhow them, from their own
beft approved authors, as many different opinions
as they could charge againft us. Here, again, a
gentleman, in the prefence of the old bifhop and
a prieft, offered me his houfe, and whole living,
with affurance of honour, wealth and employ-
ment, if I would embrace their ways. I told
them, I had an indignation of foul againft fuch
offers on fuch terms, as parting with what was

more valuable than all the world ; alleging, *What is a man profited if he gain the whole world, and lose his own foul ? or what shall a man give in exchange for his foul ?* I was sometimes told, I might have all my children if I would comply, and must never expect to have them on any other terms. I told them, my children were dearer to me than all the world, but I would not deny Christ and his truths for the having of them with me ; I would still put my trust in God, who could perform all things for me.

I am persuaded that the priest of that parish, where I kept, abhorred their sending down the heathen to commit outrages against the English, saying, it was more like committing murders, than managing a war. In my confinement in this parish, I had my undisturbed opportunities to be humbly imploring grace for ourselves, for foul and body, for his protecting presence with New-England, and his disappointing the bloody designs of enemies ; that God would be a little sanctuary to us in a land of captivity, and that our friends in New-England might have grace to make a more thankful and fruitful improvement of the means of grace than we had done ; who, by our neglects, find ourselves out of God's sanctuary.

On the twenty-first of October, 1704, I received some letters from New-England, with an account that many of our neighbours escaped out of the desolations in the fort, and that my dear wife was carried back, and decently buried : And that my eldest son, who was absent in our desolation, was sent to college, and provided for ; which occasioned thankfgiving to God in the midst of afflictions,

afflictions, and caused prayers, even in Canada, to be going daily up to Heaven for a blessing upon benefactors, showing such kindness to the desolate and afflicted. The consideration of such crafty designs to ensnare young ones, and to turn them from the simplicity of the gospel to Romish superstition, was very exercising ; sometimes they would tell me my children, sometimes my neighbours, were turned to be of their religion. Some made it their work to allure poor souls by flatteries and great promises, some threatened, some offered abusive carriage to such as refused to go to church and be present at mass. Some they industriously contrived to get married among them. A priest drew up a compendium of the Roman catholick faith, and pretended to prove it by the scriptures, telling the English, that all they required was contained in the scriptures, which they acknowledged to be the rule of faith and manners ; but it was by scriptures horribly perverted and abused. I could never come to the sight of it, (though I often earnestly entreated a copy of it), until I was on shipboard, for our voyage to New-England ; but hearing of it, I endeavoured to possess the English with their danger of being cheated with such a pretence. I understood they would tell the English that I was turned, that they might gain them to change their religion. These their endeavours to seduce to popery were very exercising to me : And in my solitariness I drew up these following sorrowful, mournful considerations, though unused to, and unskilful in poetry, yet in a plain style, for the use of some of the captives, who would some-

times

times make their secret visits to me, which, at
the desire of some of them, are here made publick.

*Some contemplations of the poor and desolate state of
the church at Deerfield.*

THE sorrows of my heart enlarged are,
Whilst I my present state with past compare.
I frequently unto God's house did go,
With christian friends, his praises forth to show.
But now, I solitary sit, both sigh and cry,
Whilst my flock's misery think on do I.
    Many, both old & young, were slain out-right ;
Some, in a bitter season, took their flight.
Some burnt to death, and others stifled were ;
The enemy no sex or age would spare.
The tender children, with their parents sad,
Are carried forth as captives, some unclad.
Some murdered in the way, unburied left,
And some, through famine, were of life bereft.
After a tedious journey, some are sold,
Some kept in heathen hands, all from Christ's fold:
By popish rage, and heath'nish cruelty,
Are banished. Yea some compell'd to be
Present at mass. Young children parted are
From parents, and such as instructors were.
Crafty designs are us'd by papists all,
In ignorance of truth, them to inthrall.
Some threat'ned are, unless they will comply,
In heathen's hands again be made to lie.
To some, large promises are made, if they
Will truths renounce, & choose their popish way.
    Oh Lord ! mine eyes on thee shall waiting be,
Till thou again turn our captivity.

Their

Their Romiſh plots, thou canſt confound ; & ſave
This little flock, this mercy I do crave.
Save us from all our ſins, and yet again
Deliver us from them who truth diſdain.

　　Lord ! for thy mercy ſake, thy cov'nant mind ;
And in thy houſe again, reſt let us find.

　　So we thy praiſes forth will ſhew, and ſpeak
Of all thy wond'rous works, yea we will ſeek
The advancement of thy great and glorious name,
Thy rich and ſovereign grace we will proclaim.

THE hearts of ſome were ready to be diſcouraged and ſink, ſaying, They were out of
ſight, and ſo out of mind. I endeavoured to
perſuade them we were not forgotten, that
undoubtedly many prayers were continually going up to heaven for us. Not long after, came
captain Livingſton, and Mr. Sheldon, with letters from his excellency our governor to the governour of Canada, about the exchange of priſoners ; which gave a revival to many, and raiſed
expectations of a return. Theſe viſits from New-
England to Canada, ſo often, greatly ſtrengthen-
ed many who were ready to faint ; and gave ſome
check to the deſigns of the papiſts to gain proſelytes. But God's time of deliverance was not
yet come ; as to ſome particular perſons, their
temptations and trials were increaſed ; and ſome
abuſed, becauſe they refuſed a compliance with
their ſuperſtitions. A young woman of our town
met with a new trial ; for on a day, a Frenchman
came into the room where ſhe was, and ſhewed
her his beads, and boaſted of them, putting them
near to her ; ſhe knocked them out of his hands

on the floor ; for which fhe was beaten, and
threatened with death, and for fome days im-
prifoned. I pleaded with God his over-ruling
this firft effay for the deliverance of fome, as a
pledge of the reft being delivered in due time. I
implored captain de Beauville, who had always
been very friendly, to intercede with the governour for the return of my eldeft daughter ; and
for his purchafing my fon Stephen from the
Indians at St. François fort ; and for liberty to
go up and fee my children and neighbours at
Montreal. Divine providence appeared to the
moderating my affliction, in that five Englifh
perfons of our town were permitted to return
with captain Livingfton, among whom went my
eldeft daughter. And my fon Stephen was redeemed, and fent to live with me : He was almoft quite naked, and very poor ; he had fuffered much among the Indians. One of the jefuits
took upon him to come to the wigwam and whip
him, on fome complaint that the fquaws had
made, that he did not work enough for them.
As to my petition for going up to Montreal to
fee my children and neighbours, it was denied ;
as my former defire of coming up to the city, before captain Livingfton's coming, was. God
granted me favour as to two of my petitions, but
yet brought me by his grace to be willing, that
he fhould glorify himfelf in difpofing of me and
mine as he pleafed, and knew to be moft for his
glory : And almoft always before any remarkable
favour, I was brought to lie down at the foot of
God, and made to be willing that God fhould
govern the world fo as might be moft for his own
honour,

honour, and brought to refign all to his holy
fovereignty : A frame of fpirit, when wrought in
me by the grace of God, giving the greateft con-
tent and fatisfaction ; and very often a fore-run-
ner of the mercy afked of God, or a plain de-
monftration, that the not obtaining my requeft
was beft for me. I had no fmall refreshing, in
having one of my children with me for four
months. And the Englifh were, many of them,
ftrengthened with hopes, that the treaty betwixt
the governments would iffue in opening a door of
efcape for all.

In Auguft Mr. Dudley and captain Vetch arrived, and great encouragements were given as to
an exchange of all in the fpring of the year :
And fome few again were fent home ; among
whom I obtained leave to fend my fon Stephen.

Upon Mr. Dudley's and captain Vetch's pe-
titioning, I was again permitted to go up to
Quebec ; but difputing with a mendicant friar,
who faid, he was an Englifhman fent from France,
to endeavour the converfion of the Englifh at
Quebec, who arrived at Canada whilft our gentlemen were there, I was, by the priefts' means,
ordered to return again to Chateauviche, and no
other reafon given, but becaufe I difcourfed with
that prieft, and their fear I fhould prevent his fuccefs amongft the captives. But God fhewed his
diflike of fuch a perfecuting fpirit ; for the very
next day, which was September 20, O. S. October 1, N. S. the feminary, a very famous build-
ing, was moft of it burnt down, occafioned by a
joiner's letting a coal of fire drop among the
fhavings. The chapel in the prieft's garden, and
the

the great crofs, were burnt down ; the library of the priefts burnt up. This feminary and another library had been burnt but about three years before. The day after my being fent away, by the priefts' means, from Quebec, at firft, there was a thunder-ftorm, and the lightning ftruck the feminary in the very place where the fire now began.

A little before Mr. Dudley's arrival, came a foldier into my landlord's houfe, barefoot and barelegged, going on a pilgrimage to Saint Anne : For, faid he, my captain, who died fome years ago, appeared to me, and told me he was in purgatory ; and told me I muft go a pilgrimage to Saint Anne, doing penance, and get a mafs faid for him, and then he fhould be delivered. Many believed him, and were much affected with it ; came and told me of it, to gain my credit of their devifed purgatory. The foldier told me, the priefts had counfelled him to undertake this pilgrimage. And, I am apt to think, ordered his calling in at my landlord's, that I might fee and fpeak with him. I laughed at the conceit, that a foldier muft be pitched upon to be fent on this errand ; but they were much difpleafed, and lamented my obftinacy, in that I would not be reclaimed from a denial of purgatory by fuch a miraculous providence.

As I was able, I fpread the cafe before God, befeeching of him to difappoint them of their expectations to profelyte any of the captives by this ftratagem ; and by the goodnefs of God, it was not very ferviceable ; for the foldier's converfation was fuch, that feveral among the French
themfelves

themselves judged it to be a forgery. And though the captain, spoken of, was the governour's lady's brother, I never more heard any concernment or care to get him out of purgatory.

One of the parish, where I lived, told me, that on the twenty-second of July, 1705, he was at Quebec, at the mendicant friar's church, on one of their feast days, in honour of a great saint of their order, and that at five o'clock mass, in the morning, near two hundred persons being present, a great grey cat brake or pushed aside some glass, entered into the church, passed along near the altar, and put out five or six candles, which were burning ; and that no one could tell which way the cat went out ; and he thought it was the devil.

When I was in the city in September, I saw two English maids, who had lived with the Indians a long time. They told me, that an Indian had died at the place where they were ; and that when sundry of his relations were together, in order to attend his burial, the dead arose, and informed them, " That at his death he went to hell, and there he saw all the Indians that had been dead since their embracing the popish religion ; and warned them to leave it off, or they would be damned too ;" and laid down dead again. They said, the Indians were frightened, and very melancholy ; but the jesuit, to whom they told this, told them it was only a delusion of the devil, to draw them away from the true religion ; adding, that he knew for certain that all those Indians who had been dead, spoken of by that Indian, were in heaven ; only one squaw was gone to

hell,

hell, who died without baptifm. Thefe maids
faid alfo, that many of the Indians much lamented
their making a war againft the Englifh, at the
inftigation of the French.

The priefts, after Mr. Dudley's going from
Canada, were ready to think their time was fhort
for gaining Englifh profelytes, and doubled their
diligence and wiles to gain over perfons to their
perfuafion. I improved all opportunities I could,
to write to the Englifh, that in that way I might
be ferviceable to them. But many or moft of my
letters, treating about religion, were intercepted,
and burnt. I had a letter fent down to me by
order of the governour, that I had liberty of
writing to my children and friends, which fhould
be continued, provided I wrote about indifferent
things, and faid nothing in them about the points
in controverfy between them and us : And if I
were fo hardy as to write letters otherwife, they
fhould endeavour to prevent their being delivered.
Accordingly, I found many of them were burnt.
But fometimes notice would be given to the
Englifh, that there were letters written, but that
they were burnt ; fo that their writing was fomewhat ufeful, though never perufed by the Englifh,
becaufe they judged thofe letters condemned
popery. Many of our letters, written from New-
England, were never delivered, becaufe of fome
expreffions about religion in them. And, as I
faid before, after Mr. Dudley's departure from
Quebec, endeavours were very vigorous to feduce.
Some were flattered with large promifes, others
were threatened, and beaten, becaufe they would
not turn. And when two Englifh women, who
had

had always oppofed their religion, were fick in the hofpital, they kept with them night and day, till they died ; and their friends kept from coming to vifit them. After their death, they gave out, that they died in the Romifh faith, and were received into their communion. Before their death, maffes were faid for them ; and they were buried in the church yard, with all their ceremonies. And after this, letters were fent into all parts, to inform the Englifh, that thefe two women turned to their religion before their death ; and that it concerned them to follow their example, for they could not be more obftinate than thofe women were, in their health, againft the Romifh faith, and yet on a death bed embraced it. They told the Englifh who lived near, that our religion was a dangerous religion to die in. But I fhall hereafter relate the juft grounds we have to think thefe things were falfehoods.

I was informed, there was an Englifh girl bid to take and wear the crofs, and crofs herfelf : She refufed ; they threatened her, and fhewed her the crofs. At length, fhe had her choice, either to crofs herfelf, and take the crofs, or be whipt, fhe chofe to be whipt ; and they made as though they would correct her ; but feeing her choofing indeed to fuffer rather than comply, they defifted, and tied the crofs about her neck. Some were taken and fhut up among their religious, and all forts of means ufed to gain them.

I received a letter from one of my neighbours, wherein he thus bewails : ' I obtained leave of my mafter to go to the Macqua fort, to fee my children, that I had not feen for a long time.

' I carried

' I carried a letter from my master, to shew that I
' had leave to come. When I came to the fort,
' I heard one of my children was in the woods. I
' went to see a boy I had there, who lived with
' one of the jesuits ; I had just asked him of his
' welfare ; he said his master would come present-
' ly ; he durst not stay to speak with me now,
' being in such awe of his master. On which I
' withdrew ; and when his master came in, I went
' and asked leave of him to speak with my child,
' and shewed him my letter. But he absolutely
' refused to let me see or speak with him ; and
' said, I had brought no letter from the govern-
' our, and would not permit me to stay in the fort,
' though I had travelled on foot near fifty miles,
' for no other errand than to see and speak with
' my children.'

The same person, with another Englishman,
last spring, obtained leave of the governour general to go to the same fort on the same errand, and
carried letters from the governour to the jesuits,
that he might be permitted to speak with his
children. The letter was delivered to the jesuits ;
who told him, his son was not at home, but gone
a hunting : Whereas he was hid from them, as he
heard afterward ; so the poor man lost his labour
a second time. These men say, that when they
returned to Montreal, one Laland, who was appointed as a spy, always to observe the motions of
the English, told them, that one of the jesuits
had come in before them, and had told the governour that the lad was gone out a hunting : And
that the Englishman, who accompanied this poor
man, went out into the woods, in hopes of finding
the

the lad ; and saw him, but the lad run away ; and that he followed him, and called after him, but he would not stop ; but holding out a gun, threatened to shoot him down, if he followed him ; and so he was discouraged, and turned back. And, says Laland, you will never leave going to see your children and neighbours, till some of you are killed. But the men told him, it was an absolute lie, let who would report it ; for they had neither seen the lad, nor did they go into the woods to search after him. They judge this was told to the governour, to prevent any English for the future going to see their children and neighbours. Some of ours say, they have been little better than absolutely promised to have their children, who are among the savages, in case they themselves would embrace popery. And that the priests had said, they had rather the children should be among the Indians, as they were, than be brought out by the French, and so. be in readiness to return for New-England.

A maid of our town was put into a religious house, among the nuns, for more than two years, and all sorts of means, by flatteries, threatenings, and abusive carriages, used to bring her to turn. They offered her money, which when refused, especially the latter part of the time, they threatened her very much ; sent for her before them, and commanded her to cross herself. She refused, they hit her a box on the ear ; bid her again, still she refused. They ordered a rod with six branches full of knots to be brought ; and when she refused, they struck her on the hands, still renewing their commands ; and she stood to her

refusals,

refusals, till her hands were filled with wales, with the blows. But one said, Beat her no more, we will give her to the Indians, if she will not turn. They pinched her arms till they were black and blue ; and made her go into their church ; and because she would not crofs herself, struck her several blows with their hands on her face. A squaw was brought in, and said, she was sent to fetch her to the Indians ; but she refused ; the squaw went away, and said, she would bring her husband with her to-morrow, and she should be carried away by force. She told me, she remembered what I told her one day, after the nuns had threatened to give her away to the Indians ; that they only said so to affright her, that they never would give her away. The nuns told her, she should not be permitted any more to speak to the English ; and that they would afflict her without giving her any rest, if she refused : But God preserved her from falling. This poor girl had many prayers going up to Heaven for her daily, and by name, because her trials were more known to some of the English, than the trials of others, who lived more remote from them.

Here might be a history by itself, of the trials and sufferings of many of our children, and young ones, who have been abused, and after separation from grown persons, made to do as they would have them.

I shall here give an account of what was done to one of my children, a boy between fifteen and sixteen years of age, two hundred miles distant from me, which occasioned grief and sorrow, that I want words to utter ; and yet kept under such

awe,

awe, that he never durſt write any thing to me,
for fear of being diſcovered in writing about religion. They threatened to put him to the Indians again, if he would not turn ; telling him,
he was never bought out of their hands, but only
ſojourned with them, but if he would turn, he
ſhould never be put into their hands any more.
The prieſts would ſpend whole days in urging
him. He was ſent to ſchool to learn to read and
write French ; the ſchool-maſter ſometimes flattered him with promiſes, if he would croſs himſelf ; then threatened him if he would not. But
when he ſaw flattering promiſes of rewards, and
threatenings, were ineffectual, he ſtruck him with
a ſtick he had in his hand ; and when he ſaw
that would not do, he made him get down on his
knees about an hour ; and then came and bid
him make the ſign of the croſs, and that without
any delay ; he ſtill refuſed. Then he gave him
a couple of ſtrokes, with a whip he had in his
hand ; which whip had three branches, and
about twelve great knots tied in it. And again
bid him make the ſign of the croſs ; and if it
was any ſin, he would bear it himſelf : And ſaid
alſo, You are afraid you ſhall be changed if you
do it : But (ſaid he) you will be the ſame, your
fingers will not be changed. And after he had
made him ſhed many tears, under his abuſes and
threatenings, he told him, he would have it done :
And ſo through cowardice and fear of the whip,
he made the ſign. And did ſo for ſeveral days
together, with much ado, he was brought to croſs
himſelf. And then the maſter told him, he
would have it done without his particular bidding
him.

him. And when he came to say his lesson, and
crossed not himself, the master said, have you forgot what I bid you do ? No, sir, said he ; then
the schoolmaster said, Down on your knees ; and
so kept him for an hour and half, till school was
done ; and so did for about a week. When he
saw this would not do, he took the whip, What,
will not you do it, (said he), I will make you :
And so again frighted him to a compliance.
After this, he commanded him to go to the
church : When he refused, he told him, he would
make him. And one morning sent four of the
biggest boys of the school, to draw him by force
to mass. These, with other severities and witty
stratagems, were used ; and I utterly ignorant of
any attempt made upon him, to bring him to
change his religion. His fear was such, that he
never durst write any of these things, left his letters should fall into their hands, and he should
again be delivered to the Indians. Hearing of
an opportunity of writing to him by one of the
parish where I was, going up to Montreal, I
wrote a letter to him, and had by him a letter
from my son ; which I shall here insert.

" *Honoured Father*,

" I HAVE received your letter, bearing date
January 11, 1705,6 ; for which I give you many
thanks, with my duty and my brother's. I am
sorry you have not received all the letters I have
written to you ; as I have not received all yours.
According to your good counsel, I do almost
every day read something of the bible, and so
strengthen my faith. As to the captives newly
brought, Lancaster is the place of two of them,
                                                    and

and Marlborough that of the third ; the governour of Montreal has them all three.   There is
other news that will feem more ftrange to you :
That two Englifh women, who in their life time
were dreadfully fet againft the catholick religion,
did on their death bed embrace it.   The one
Abigail Turbet, the other of them Efther Jones,
both of them known to you.   Abigail Turbet
fent for Mr. Meriel the Sabbath before fhe died ;
and faid (many a time upon feveral following
days) that fhe committed her foul into his hands,
and was ready to do whatever he pleafed.   She
defired him to go to the chapel St. Anne, and
there to fay a holy mafs for her, that fhe might
have her fins pardoned, and the will of the Lord
accomplifhed upon her.   Her coufin, Mrs. Bad-
fton, now Stilfon, afked her, whether fhe fhould
be willing to do as fhe faid ; fhe anfwered, yes.
And upon the Tuefday fhe was taken into the
catholick church, in the prefence of John Laland,
and madam Grizalem, an Englifh woman, and
Mrs. Stilfon, alfo with many French people befides.   She was anointed with oil on the fame
day, according to her will then.   Upon the
Wednefday following, an image of Chrift crucifi-
ed was brought to her ; fhe caufed it to be fet
up over againft her, at the curtains of her bed,
and looked continually upon the fame ; and alfo
a little crucifix was broughtunto her ; fhe took it,
and kiffed it, and laid it upon her ftomach.   She
did alfo make the fign of the crofs upon herfelf,
when fhe took any meat or drink.   She promifed to God, that if fhe fhould recover, fhe would
go to the mafs every day : She having on her
F   hand

hand a crucifix, said, Oh, my Lord, that I should have known thee so late ! She did also make a prayer to the Virgin Mary, the two last days of the week. She could utter no word, but by kissing the crucifix, and endeavouring to crofs herself, she gave an evidence of her faith. She died on Saturday the 24th of November, at three o'clock in the afternoon. The next day, the priest did commend that woman's foul to the prayers of the congregation in the mass ; in the afternoon she was honourably buried in the church yard, next to the church, close to the body of the justice Pefe's wife ; all the people being prefent at her funeral. The fame day, in the evening, Mr. Meriel, with an English woman, went to Efther Jones ; she did at firft difdain ; but a little after, she confeffed there were feven facraments, Chrift's body prefent, the facrament of the mafs, the inequality of power among the paftors of the church ; and being returned to wait by her all night long, he read and expounded to her fome part of the catholick confeffion of faith to her fatisfaction. About midnight he afked her, whether she might not confefs her fins ; I doubt not but I may, faid she : And two hours after, she made unto him a fervent confeffion of all the fins of her whole life : When he faid, he was to offer Chrift to his father for her, she liked it very well. The fuperior of the nuns being come in to fee her, she now defired that she might receive Chrift's body before she died. She did also show Mrs. Stilfon a great mind to receive the facrament of extreme unction, and faid, that if ever she should recover and get home, she

she would reproach the ministers for their neg-
lecting that sacrament, so plainly commanded
by St. James. In the afternoon, after she had
begged pardon for her wavering, and the catholick confession of faith was read aloud to her, in
the hearing of Mr. Crafton, Mrs. Stilson, and
another English woman, she owned the same.
About seven o'clock the same day, she said to
Mr. Dubison, shall not they give me the holy
communion ? But her tongue was then so thick
that she could hardly swallow any thing. She
was then anointed with holy oil : But before, she
said to Mr. Meriel, why have you not yet, sir, for-
given my sins ? In the night following, that priest,
and Mr. Dubison, were continually by her ; and
sometimes praying to God in her name, and praying to the Virgin Mary, and other saints. She
said also, I believe all : I am very glad Christ
was offered to his Father for me. Six or seven
hours before she died, a crucifix was showed to
her by Mr. Dubison ; she took it, and laid it
upon her heart, and kissed it ; and then the nuns
hanged it with a pair of beads upon her neck.
A little before she died, Mr. Dubison asked her
to pray for him in heaven ; she promised him :
So she gave up the ghost, at ten of the clock, the
27th of November, whilst the high mass was
saying ; she was soon commended to the prayers.
On the fourth day of the week following she was
buried, after the mass had been said for her. She
was laid by Abigail Turbet. Jan. 23, 1705,6."

I HAVE here transcribed the letter in the
very words of it, without the least alteration :
The

The fame for fubftance was fent to feveral other captives. When I had this letter, I prefently knew it to be of Mr. Meriel's compofing : But the meffenger, who brought the letter, brought word that my fon had embraced their religion. Afterwards, when fome blamed him for letting me know of it, becaufe (they faid) they feared my forrow would fhorten my days ; he told me, he thought with himfelf, that if he was in my cafe he fhould be willing to know the worft, and therefore told me, as he would have defired to have known if in my place. I thanked him, acknowledging it a favour to let me know of it ;. but the news was ready to overwhelm me with grief and forrow. I made my complaint to God, and mourned before him ; forrow and anguifh took hold upon me. I afked of God to direct me what to do, and how to write, and find out an opportunity of conveying a letter to him ; and committed this difficulty to his providence. I now found a greater oppofition to a patient, quiet, humble refignation to the will of God than I fhould otherwife have known, if not fo tried. Here I thought of my afflictions and trials ; my wife and two children killed, and many of my neighbours ; and myfelf, fo many of my children and friends in a popifh captivity, feparated from our children, not capable to come to them to inftruct them in the way they ought to go ; and cunning, crafty enemies, ufing all their fubtilty to infinuate into young ones, fuch principles as would be pernicious. I thought with myfelf how happy many others were, in that they had their children with them, under all advantages to

bring

bring them up in the nurture and admonition of
the Lord ; whilst we were separated one from
another, and our children in great peril of embracing damnable doctrines. Oh ! that all parents, who read this history, would bless God for
the advantages they have of educating their
children, and faithfully improve it ! I mourned
when I thought with myself that I had one child
with the Macquas, a second turned to popery,
and a little child, of six years of age, in danger
from a child to be instructed in popery ; and
knew full well that all endeavours would be used
to prevent my seeing or speaking with them.
But in the midst of all these, God gave me a secret hope, that he would magnify his power and
free grace, and disappoint all their crafty designs.
When I looked on the right hand and on the
left, all refuge failed me, and none shewed any
care for my soul. But God brought that word
to uphold me ; *Who is able to do exceeding abundantly above what we can ask or think.* As also
that, *Is any thing too hard for God ?* I prayed to
God to direct me ; and wrote very short the first
time, and in general terms, fearing lest if I should
write about things in controversy, my letters
would not come to him. I therefore addressed
him with the following letter.

  " *Son Samuel,*

  " YOURS of January 23, I received, and with
it had the tidings that you had made an abjuration
of the Protestant faith for the Romish : News
that I heard with the most distressing, afflicting,
sorrowful spirit that ever I heard any news. Oh !
I pity you, I mourn over you day and night !

F 2   Oh !

Oh! I pity your weaknefs, that through the craftinefs of man you are turned from the fimplicity of the gofpel! I perfuade myfelf you have done it through ignorance. Oh! why have you neglected to afk a father's advice in an affair of fo great importance as the change of religion! God knows that the catechifm, in which I inftructed you, is according to the word of God; and fo will be found in the day of judgment. Oh! confider and bethink yourfelf what you have done! And whether you afk me or not, my poor child, I cannot but pray for you, that you may be recovered out of the fnare you are taken in. Read the bible, pray in fecret; make Chrift's righteoufnefs your only plea before God, for juftification: Beware of all immorality, and of profaning God's Sabbaths. Let a father's advice be afked for the future, in all things of weight and moment. What is a man profited if he gain the whole world, and lofe his own foul? Or what fhall a man give in exchange for his foul? I defire to be humbled under the mighty hand of God thus afflicting of me. I would not do as you have done for ten thoufand worlds. My heart aches within me, but I will yet wait upon the Lord; to him will I commit your cafe day and night: He can perform all things for me and mine; and can yet again recover you from your fall. He is a God forgiving iniquity, tranfgreffion and fin: To the Lord our God belong forgiveneffes, though we have rebelled. I charge you not to be inftrumental to enfnare your poor brother Warham, or any other, and fo add fin to fin. Accept of my love, and do not forfake a
father's

father's advice, who above all things defires that your foul may be faved in the day of the Lord."

WHAT I mournfully wrote, I followed with my poor cries to God in heaven to make effectual, to caufe in him a confideration of what he had done. God faw what a proud heart I had, and what need I had to be fo anfwered out of the whirlwind, that I might be humbled before him. Not having any anfwer to my letter for fome weeks, I wrote the following letter, as I was enabled of God, and fent to him by a faithful hand ; which, by the blefling of God, was made effectual for his good, and the good of others, who had fallen to popery ; and for the eftablifhing and ftrengthening of others to refift the effays of the adverfary to truth. God brought good out of this evil, and made what was defigned to promote their intereft, an occafion of fhame to them.

" *Son Samuel,*

" I HAVE waited till now for an anfwer from you, hoping to hear from you, why you made an abjuration of the Proteftant faith for the Romifh. But fince you continue to neglect to write to me about it, as you neglected to take any advice or counfel from a father, when you did it, I cannot forbear writing again, and making fome reflections on the letter you wrote me laft, about the two women. It feems to me, from thofe words of Abigail Turbet's, in your letter, or rather of Mr. Meriel's, which you tranfcribed for him—— [Abigail Turbet fent for Mr. Meriel, committed her foul into his hand, and was ready to do whatfoever he pleafed]——I fay, it feems rational to believe

believe, that she had not the use of her reason ; it is an expression to be abhorred by all who have any true sense of religion. Was Mr. Meriel a God, a Christ? Could he bear to hear such words and not reject them; replying, " do not commit your soul into my hands, but see that you commit your soul into the hands of God through Christ Jesus, and do whatever God commands you in his holy word. As for me, I am a creature, and cannot save your soul ; but will tell you of Acts iv. 12. *Neither is there salvation in any other ; for there is no other name under heaven given among men, whereby we must be saved.*" Had he been a faithful minister of Jesus Christ, he would have said, " It is an honour due to Christ alone. The holy apostle says, *Now unto him that is able to keep you, and present you faultless before the presence of his glory, with exceeding joy, to the only wise God our Saviour, be glory, and majesty, dominion and power, both now and ever, amen.*" Jude, 24, 25, verses. As to what you write about praying to the Virgin Mary, and other saints, I make this reply, Had Mr. Meriel done his duty, he would have said to them, as 1 John, ii. 1, 2. *If any man sin, we have an advocate with the Father, Jesus Christ the righteous ; and he is the propitiation for our sins.* The scriptures say, *There is one God, and one mediator between God and man, the man Christ Jesus.* Yea, Christ said, go and preach, *He that believeth and is baptized, shall be saved.* The apostle, in Gal. i. 8. saith, *But though we or an angel from heaven preach any other gospel unto you, than that we have preached to you, let him be accursed.* They never preached, that we should pray to the

Virgin Mary, or other faints. As you would be saved, hear what the apostle faith, Heb. iv. 13, &c. *Neither is there any creature that is not manifest in his sight ; but all things are naked, and open unto the eyes of him with whom we have to do. Seeing then that we have a great high priest that is entered into the heavens, Jesus the son of God, let us hold fast our profession : For we have not an high priest that cannot be touched with the feelings of our infirmities, but was in all points tempted like as we are, yet without sin ; let us therefore come boldly unto the throne of grace, that we may obtain mercy, and find grace to help in time of need.* Which words do hold forth, how that Christ Jesus is in every respect qualified to be a mediator and interceffor ; and I am sure they cannot be applied to any mere creature, to make them capable of our religious truft. When Roman catholicks have faid all they can, they are not able to prove, that the faints in heaven have a knowledge of what prayers are directed to them. Some fay they know then one way, others fay they have the knowledge of them in another way : And that which they have fixed upon as moft probable to them, is, that they know of them from their beholding the face of God ; feeing God, they know thefe prayers : But this is a great miftake. Though the faints fee and know God in a glorious manner, yet they have not an infinite knowledge ; and it does no ways follow, that becaufe they fee God, they know all prayers that are directed to them upon the earth. And God has no where in his word told us, that the faints have fuch a knowledge. Befides, were it a thing poffible for them to have

a knowledge

a knowledge of what prayers are directed to them, it does not follow that they are to be prayed to, or have religious honour conferred upon them. The Romanists can neither give one scripture precept or example for praying to them ; but God has provided a mediator, who knows all our petitions, and is faithful and merciful enough ; and we have both scripture precept and example, to look to him as our mediator and advocate with the Father.   Further, it cannot be proved that it is consistent with the saints being creatures, as well as with their happiness, to have a knowledge of prayers from all parts of the world at the same time, from many millions together, about things so vastly differing one from another : And then to present those supplications for all that look to them, is not humility, but will-worship.   Col. ii. 18. *Let no man beguile you of your reward, in a voluntary humility, worshipping of angels,* verse 23. *Which things indeed have a shew of wisdom and will-worship, and humility.*   For what humility can it be, to distrust the way that God has provided and encouraged us to come to him in, and impose upon God a way of our own devising ? Was not God angry with Jeroboam for imposing upon him after such a sort ? 1 Kings, xii. 33. *So he offered upon the altar which he had made in Bethel, the fifth day of the eighth month, which he devised of his own heart.* Therefore Christ saith, Mark vii. 7. *Howbeit, in vain do they worship me, teaching for doctrines the commandments of men.* Before the coming of Christ, and his entering into heaven as an intercessor ; Heb. vii. 25. *Wherefore he is able to save them to the uttermost*
that

*that come to God by him, seeing he ever liveth to make
intercession for them* ; I say, before Chrift's entering into heaven as an interceffor, there is not
one word of any prayer to faints ; and what reafon can be given that now there is need of fo
many faints to make interceffion, when Chrift as
a prieft is entered into heaven to make interces-
fion for us ? The anfwer that the Romanifts give
is a very fable and falfehood : Namely, that there
were no faints in heaven till after the refurrection
and afcenfion of Chrift, but were referved in a
place called Limbus Patrum, and fo had not the
beatifical vifion. See Gen. v. 24. *Enoch walked
with God, and was not, for God took him.* If he
was not taken into heaven, what can be the fenfe
of thofe words, *for God took him ?* Again, 2 Kings,
ii. 1. When the Lord would take up Elijah into
heaven by a whirlwind, verfe 11. *There appeared
a chariot of fire and horfes of fire, and parted them
both afunder, and Elijah went up by a whirlwind
into heaven.* Muft the truth of the fcripture be
called in queftion to uphold their notions ? Befides, it is not confiftent with reafon to fuppofe,
that Enoch and Elias, inftead of having a peculiar privilege vouchfafed to them, for their em-
inency in holinefs, fhould be lefs happy for fo
long a time than the reft of the faints deceafed,
who are glorified in heaven ; which muft be, if
they are yet kept, and muft be, till the day of
judgment out of heaven, and the beatifical vifion,
in an earthly paradife, according to fome of the
Romanifts ; or in fome other place, they know
not where, according to others. Religious worfhip is not to be given to the creature, Mat. iv.
9, 10,

9, 10, and faith, *All thefe things will I give thee, if thou wilt fall down and worfhip me.* Then faith Jefus to him, *Get thee hence, Satan; for it is written, thou fhalt worfhip the Lord thy God, and him only fhalt thou ferve.* That phrafe, *and him only fhalt thou ferve,* excludes all creatures. Rev. xxii. 8, 9. *I fell down to worfhip before the feet of the angel, which fhewed me thefe things; then faith he to me, fee thou do it not, for I am thy fellow fervant, and of thy brethren the prophets, and of them which keep the fayings of this book, worfhip God.* Which plainly fhews, that God only is to be worfhipped with a religious worfhip. None can think that Saint John intended to give the higheft divine worfhip to the angel, who faith, *Do not fall down and worfhip me; it is God's due, worfhip God.* So Acts x. 25, 26. *As Peter was coming in, Cornelius met him and fell down at his feet, and worfhipped him; but Peter took him up, faying, ftand up, I myfelf alfo am a man.* See alfo Lev. xix. 10. The words of the fecond commandment (which the Romanifts either leave out, or add to the firft commandment, faying, *Thou fhalt have no other gods before me,* adding, &c.) I fay the words of the fecond commandment are, *Thou fhalt not make to thyfelf any graven image, or any likenefs of any thing that is in heaven above, or that is in the earth beneath, or that is in the waters under the earth; thou fhalt not bow down thyfelf to them nor ferve them, for I the Lord thy God am a jealous God,* &c. Thefe words being inferted in the letter which came from your brother Eleazer, in New-England, the laft fummer, was the caufe of the letters being fent down from Montreal, and not given to you,

when

when so near you, as I suppose, there being no
other clause of the letter that could be objected against, and the reason why found at Quebec,
when I sent it to you a second time, enclosed in
a letter written by myself.   The brazen serpent,
made by divine appointment as a type of Christ,
when abused to superstition, was by reforming
Hezekiah broken in pieces.   As to what the
Romanists plead about the lawfulness of image
and saint worship, from those likenesses of things
made in Solomon's temple, it is nothing to the
purpose.   We do not say it is not lawful to make
or have a picture ; but those carved images were
not, in the temple, to be adored, bowed down to,
or worshipped.   There is no manner of consequence, that because there were images made in
Solomon's temple that were not adored and worshipped, that therefore it is now lawful to make
and fall down before images, and pray to them,
and so worship them.

" Religious worshipping of saints cannot be
defended from, but is forbidden, in the scriptures ;
and for fear of losing their disciples, the Romanists keep away from them the bible, and oblige
them to believe as they say they must believe ;
as though there was no use to be made of our
reason about our souls ; and yet the Bereans were
counted noble for searching the scriptures, to see
whether the things preached by Saint Paul were
so or not.   They dare not allow you liberty to
speak with your father, or others, for fear their
errors should be discovered to you.   Again, you
write, " that Esther Jones confessed that there
was an inequality of power among the pastors of

G   the

the church." An argument to convince the world, that becaufe the priefts, in fallacious ways, caufed a woman, diftempered with a very high fever, if not diftracted, to fay, fhe confeffed there was an inequality of power among the paftors of the church, therefore all the world are obliged to believe that there is a pope. An argument to be fent from Dan to Beerfheba, every where, where any Englifh captives are, to gain their belief of a pope. Can any rational man think that Chrift, in the 16th chapter of Matthew, gave Saint Peter fuch a power as the papifts fpeak of ; or that the difciples fo underftood Chrift ? When immediate-ly there arofe a difpute among them, who fhould be the greateft in the kingdom of heaven ? Matth. xviii. 1. *At the fame time came the difciples of Jefus, faying, who is the greateft in the kingdom of heaven ?* The rock fpoken of in the 16th of Matthew, not the perfon of Peter, but the con-feffion made by him, and the fame power is given to all the difciples, if you compare one fcripture with another ; not one word in any place of fcripture of fuch a vicarfhip power as of a pope, nor any folid foundation of proof that Peter had a greater authority than the reft of the apoftles. 1 Cor. iv. 6. *That you might learn in us, not to think of men above that which is written.* Yea, the apoftle condemns them, 1 Cor. i. 12. for their contentions, *One faying, I am of Paul, I of Apollos, and I of Cæphas ,* no more of Peter's being a foundation than any of the reft. *For we are built upon the foundation of the apoftles and prophets, Jefus Chrift himfelf being the chief corner ftone.* Not one word in any of Peter's epiftles, fhowing

that

that he had greater power than the other apostles. Nay, if the scriptures give any preference, it is to Saint Paul rather than Saint Peter. 1 Cor. iii. 10. *According to the grace of God which is given to me, as a wise master builder I have laid the foundation.* 1 Cor. v. 3, 4. *For I verily as absent in body, but present in spirit, have judged already, as though I were present, concerning him that hath so done this deed. In the name of our Lord Jesus Christ, when ye are gathered together, and my spirit, with the power of our Lord Jesus Christ,* &c. 1 Cor. vii. 1. *Now concerning the things whereof ye wrote to me ;* application made not to Saint Peter, but Paul, for the decision of a controversy or scruple. 1 Cor. xi. 2. *Now I praise you, brethren, that you remember me in all things, and keep the ordinance as I delivered them to you.* Either those spoken of, Acts xv. or in his ministry and epistles, 2 Cor. ii. 10. *For your sake, forgave I it, in the person of Christ.* 2 Cor. xi. 28. *That which cometh upon me daily, the care of all the churches.* 2 Cor. xii. 11, 12. *For in nothing am I behind the very chiefest of the apostles, though I be nothing. Truly the signs of an apostle were wrought among you in all patience, in signs and wonders, and mighty deeds ;* and in other places. Again, if you consult Acts xv. where you have an account of the first synod or council, you will find that the counsel or sentence of the apostle James is followed, verse 19. Wherefore my sentence is, &c. not a word that Saint Peter was chief. Again, you find Peter himself sent forth by the other apostles, Acts viii. 14. *The apostles sent unto them, Peter and John.* When the church of the Jews found fault with Peter, for

going

going in to the Gentiles when he went to Cornelius, he does not say, Why do you queftion me, or call me to an account, I am Chrift's vicar on earth. When Paul reproved Peter, Gal. ii. he does not defend himfelf, by mentioning an infallibility in himfelf as Chrift's vicar, or reprove Paul for his boldnefs.

" The Roman catholick church cannot be a true church of Chrift, in that it makes laws directly contrary to the laws and commands of Chrift : As for example, in with-holding the wine or the cup from the laity, in the Lord's fupper ; whereas Chrift commands the fame to drink who were to eat. Their evafion, that the blood is in the body, and fo they partake of both in eating, is a great fallacy, built on a falfe foundation of tranfubftantiation. For when men eat, they cannot be faid to drink, which Chrift commands, for Chrift commands that we *take the cup and drink*, which is not done in eating ; befides, the priefts themfelves will not be fo put off. The words, *this is my body*, do only intend, *this doth fignify or reprefent my body*, which will appear if you compare fcripture with fcripture ; for after the confecration, the Holy Ghoft calls it bread, and the fruit of the vine. Exod. xii. 11. *It is the Lord's paffover ;* that is, it reprefents it. In all the evangelifts, you read of killing and eating the paffover, a few lines or verfes before thefe words, *this is my body*, which plainly fhow, that our Saviour, in the fame way of figurative expreffion, fpeaks of the gofpel facrament. If thefe words were taken as the Romanifts expound them, he muft eat his own body himfelf, whole and entire fire in his own hands ; and after that, each one of the disciples eat him entire, and yet he set at the table whole, untouched, at the same time : contradictions impossible to be defended by any rational arguments. Yea, his whole body must be now in heaven and in a thousand other places, and in the mouth of every communicant at the same time, and that both as a broken and un-broken sacrifice, and be subject to putrefaction. Christ is said to be a door, a true vine, a way, a rock. What work shall we make if we expound these in a literal manner, as the Romanists do, when they say, *this is my body,* means the real body of Christ in the eucharist ? It is said, 1 Cor. x. 4. *And did all drink the same spiritual drink : For they drank of that spiritual Rock that followed them : And that rock was Christ.* Was Christ lit-erally a rock, think you ? Yea, it is absurd to believe, that a priest, uttering a few words over a wafer not above an inch square, can make it a God, or the body of Christ entire, as it was offered on the cross. It is a blasphemy to pretend to a power of making God at their pleasure ; and then eat him, and give him to others to be eaten, or shut him up in their altars : That they can utter the same words, and make a God or not make a God, according to their intention, and that the people are obliged to believe that it is God, and so adore it, when they never hear any word of consecration, nor know the priest's intention.

" As to what you write about the holy mass, I reply, it is wholly an human invention ; not a word of such a sacrifice in the whole bible ; its being a sacrifice propitiatory daily to be offered,

is

is contrary to the holy scriptures. Heb. vii. 27. *Who needeth not daily, as those high-priests, to offer up sacrifice first for his own sins, and then for the people's : For this he did once, when he offered up himself.* And yet the Romanists say, there is need that he be offered up as a sacrifice to God every day. Heb. ix. 12. *By his own blood he entered in once into the holy p'ace, having obtained eternal redemption for us.* ver. 25, 26, 27, 28. *Nor yet that he should offer himself often, as the high-priest entereth into the holy place, every year, with the blood of others : For then must he often have suffered since the foundation of the world. But now once, in the end of the world, hath he appeared to put away sin by the sacrifice of himself. As it is appointed unto men once to die, but after this the judgment ; so Christ was once offered to bear the sins of many.* Heb. x. 10. *By which will we are sanctified, through the offering of the body of Jesus Christ once for all.* ver. 12. *But this man, after he had offered one sacrifice for sins, forever sat down on the right-hand of God.* ver. 14. *For by one offering he hath perfected forever them that are sanctified.* By which scriptures you may see, that the mass is not of divine appointment, but an human invention. Their evasion of a bloody and an unbloody sacrifice, is a sham ; the holy scriptures speak not one word of Christ's being offered as a sacrifice propitiatory, after such a sort as they call an unbloody sacrifice. All the ceremonies of the mass are human inventions, which God never commanded.

" As to what is in the letter about praying for the women after their death, it is very ridiculous. For as the tree falls, so it lies ; as death leaves,
judgment

judgment will find. No change after death from an afflicted to a happy place and state. Purgatory is a phantasm, for enriching the clergy, and impoverishing the laity. The notion of it is a fatal snare to many souls, who sin with hopes of easily getting priestly absolutions at death, and buying off torments with their money. The soul at death goes immediately to judgment, and so to heaven or hell. No authentick place of scripture mentions so much as one word of any such place or state. Mr. Meriel told me, " If I found one error in our religion, it was enough to cause me to disown our whole religion." By his argument, you may see what reason you have to avoid that religion that is so full of errors. Bethink yourself, and consult the scriptures, if you can get them : (I mean the bible). Can you think their religion is right, when they are afraid to let you have an English bible ? Or to speak with your father, or other of your christian neighbours, for fear they should give you such convictions of truth that they cannot remove ? Can that religion be true, that cannot bear an examination from the scriptures, which are a perfect rule in matters of faith ? Or that must be upheld by ignorance, especially ignorance of the holy scriptures ?

" These things have I written, as in my heart I believe. I long for your recovery, and will not cease to pray for it. I am now a man of a sorrowful spirit, and look upon your fall as the most aggravating circumstance of my afflictions, and am persuaded that no pains will be wanting to prevent me from seeing or speaking with you ; but I know that God's grace is all-sufficient.

He

He is able to do exceeding abundantly above what I can afk or think. Do not give way to difcouragement as to a return to New-England ; read over what I have written, and keep it with you if you can ; you have no friend on earth that wifheth your eternal falvation more heartily than your father. I long to fee and fpeak with you, but I never forget you ; my love to you, and to your brother and fifter, and to all our fellow-prifoners. Let me hear from you as often as you can. I hope God will appear for us before it be long.

" There are a great many other things in the letter, which deferve to be refuted ; but I fhall be too tedious in remarking on them all at once : Yet would not pafs over that paffage in the letter in which Efther Jones confeffed that there were feven facraments. To which I anfwer, That fome of the moft learned of the Romifh religion confeffed, (without the diftracting pains of a violent fever), and left it upon record in print, that it cannot be convincingly made out from the fcripture, that there are feven facraments, and that their moft inconteftable proof is from tradition, and by their traditions they might have found feventeen as well as feven ; confidering that four popes, fucceffively, fpent their lives in purging and correcting old authors. But no man can, out of the holy fcriptures, prove any more than two facraments of divine inftitution, under the New-Teftament, namely, baptifm and the Lord's fupper. If you make the fcriptures a perfect rule of faith, as you ought to do, you cannot believe as the Romifh church believers. Oh !

fee

fee that you fanctify the Lord himfelf in your heart, and make him your fear and your dread. Fear not them that can kill the body, and after that have no more that they can do ; but rather fear him that has power to deftroy foul and body in hell fire.   The Lord have mercy upon you, and fhew you mercy, for the worthinefs and righteoufnefs fake of Jefus Chrift, our great and glorious Redeemer and Advocate, who makes interceffion for tranfgreffors.   My prayers are daily offered to God for you, for your brother and fifter, yea for all my children, and fellow prifoners.

" I am your afflicted and forrowful father,

" JOHN WILLIAMS.

" Chateauviche, March 22, 1706."

GOD, who is glorioufly free and rich in his grace to vile finners, was pleafed to blefs poor and weak means for the recovery of my child fo taken, and gave me to fee, that he did not fay to the houfe of Jacob, Seek you me in vain.   Oh ! that every reader would in ever difficulty make him their refuge ; he is a hopeful ftay.   To alleviate my forrow, I received the following letter in anfwer to mine.

" *Honoured Father*,   *Montreal, May* 12, 1706.

" I RECEIVED your letter which you fent by ——, which good letter I thank you for ; and for the good counfel which you gave me : I defire to be thankful for it, and hope it will be for the good of my foul.   I may fay as in the pfalms ; *The forrows of death compaffed me, and the pains of hell gat hold on me : I found trouble and forrow, then called I upon the name of the Lord : O Lord, I befeech*

feech thee, deliver my foul! Gracious is the Lord and righteous, yea our God is merciful. As for what you afk me about my making an abjuration of the proteftant faith for the Romifh, I durft not write fo plain to you as I would, but hope to fee and difcourfe with you. I am forry for the fin I have committed in changing of religion, for which I am greatly to blame. You may know that Mr. Meriel, the fchool-mafter, and others, were continually at me about it ; at laft I gave over to it ; for which I am very forry. As for that letter you had from me, it was a letter I tranfcribed for Mr. Meriel : And for what he faith about Abigail Turbet, and Efther Jones, no body heard them but he, as I underftand. I defire your prayes to God for me, to deliver me from my fins. Oh remember me in your prayers ! I am your dutiful fon, ready to take your counfel.

"SAMUEL WILLIAMS."

THIS prieft, Mr. Meriel, has brought many letters to him, and bid him write them over and fend them, and fo he has done for many others. By this, as alfo by Mrs. Stilfon's faying, "She does not think that either of thefe women did change their religion before their death ;" and alfo, "oftentimes during their ficknefs, whilft they had the ufe of their reafon, they protefted againft the Romifh religion and faith," it is evident that thefe women never died papifts, but that it was a wily ftratagem of the priefts to advance their religion : For letters were fent immediately, after their death, to ufe this as a perfuafive argument to gain others. But God in his
providence

providence gave farther conviction of their fal-
laciousness in this matter.

For the last summer, one Biggilow, of Marlborough, a captive at Montreal, was very sick in
the hospital, and, in the judgment of all, with a
sickness to death.   Then the priests and others
gave out, that he was turned to be of their religion,
and taken into their communion : But, contrary to
their expectation, he was brought back from the
gates of death, and would comply with none of
their rites ; saying, that whilst he had the use of
his reason, he never spake any thing in favour of
their religion ; and that he never disowned the
protestant faith, nor would he now.   So that they
were silenced and put to shame.   There is no
reason to think that these two women were any
more papists than he ; but they are dead, and
cannot speak.   One of the witnesses, spoken of
in the fore-mentioned letter, told me, she knew
of no such thing, and said Mr. Meriel told her,
that he never heard a more fervent and affection-
ate prayer than one which Esther Jones made a
little before her death.   I am verily persuaded,
that he calls that prayer to God, so full of affection and confession, the confession made by her
of the sins of her whole life.   These two women
always in their health, and so in their sickness,
opposed all popish principles, as all that knew
them can testify, so long as they could be permitted to go and speak with them.   One of these
women was taken from the eastward, and the
other, namely, Esther Jones, from Northampton.

In the beginning of March, 1706, Mr. Sheldon came again to Canada, with letters from
his

his excellency our governour, at which time I
was a few days at Quebec.   And when I was
there, one night about ten o'clock, there was an
earthquake, that made a report like a cannon,
and made the houfes to tremble : It was heard
and felt many leagues, all along the ifland of St.
Laurence, and other places.   When Mr. Sheldon came the fecond time, the adverfaries did
what they could to retard the time of our return,
to gain time to feduce our young ones to popery.
Such were fent away who were judged ungain-
able, and moft of the younger fort ftill kept.
Some were ftill flattered with promifes of reward ; and great effays made to get others married among them.   One was debauched, and
then in twenty-four hours of time publifhed,
taken into their communion and married ; but
the poor foul has had time fince to lament her
fin and folly, with a bitter cry ; and afks your
prayers, that God of his fovereign grace would
yet bring her out of the horrible pit fhe has
thrown herfelf into.   Her name was Rachael
Storer, of Wells.

In April, one Zebediah Williams, of our town,
died : He was a very hopeful and pious young
man, who carried himfelf fo in his captivity, as
to edify feveral of the Englifh, and recover one
fallen to popery, taken the laft war ; though fome
were enraged againft him on thefe accounts ; yet
even the French, where he fojourned, and with
whom he converfed, would fay he was a good
man : One that was very prayerful to God, and
ftudious and painful in reading the holy fcriptures : A man of a good underftanding. and de-
                                                    firable

firable conversation. In the beginning of his
last sickness, he made me a visit, (before he went
to the hospital at Quebec.), as he had several
times before, to my great satisfaction, and our
mutual consolation and comfort in our captivity.
He lived not above two miles from me, over
the river, at the island of St. Laurence, about six
weeks or two months. After his death, the
French told me, Zebediah was gone to hell, and
damned : For, said they, he has appeared, since
his death, to one Joseph Egerly, an Englishman,
who was taken the last war, in flaming fire, telling him, " he was damned for refusing to embrace the Romish religion, when such pains were
used to bring him to the true faith, and for being
instrumental to draw him away from the Romish
communion, forsaking the mass ; and was therefore now come to advertise him of his danger."
I told them, I judged it to be a popish lie ; saying, I bless God our religion needs no lies to uphold, maintain, and establish it, as theirs did.
But they affirmed it to be true, telling me, how
God approved of their religion, and witnessed
miraculously against ours. But I still told them,
I was persuaded his soul was in heaven, and that
these reports were only devised fables to seduce
souls. For several weeks they affirmed it, telling
me, that all who came over the river from the
island affirmed it to be a truth. I begged of God
to blast this hellish design of theirs, so that in the
issue it might be to render their religion more
abominable, and that they might not gain one
soul by such a stratagem. After some weeks
had passed in such assertions, there came one into

H   my

my landlord's houfe, affirming it to be a truth reported of Zebediah, faying, Jofeph Egerly had been over the river, and told one of our neighbours this ftory. After a few hours I faw that neighbour, and afked him whether he had feen Egerly lately ; he faid, yes ; what news told he to you ? None, faid he. Then I told him what was affirmed as a truth ; he anfwered, Egerly faid nothing like this to him, and he was perfuaded he would have told him, if there had been any truth in it. About a week after this, came one John Boult from the ifland of St. Laurence, a lad taken from Newfoundland, a very ferious, fober lad, of about feventeen years of age ; he had often before came over with Zebediah to vifit me. At his coming in, he much lamented the lofs of Zebediah, and told me, " That for feveral weeks they had told him the fame ftory, affirming it to be a truth, and that Egerly was fo awakened by it, as to go again to mafs every day ;" urging him, " fince God, in fuch a miraculous way, offered fuch conviction of the truth of their religion, and the falfhood and danger of ours, to come over to their religion, or elfe his damnation would be dreadfully aggravated." He faid, " he could have no reft for them day and night," but (faid he) " I told them their religion was contrary to the word of God, and therefore I would not embrace it ; and that I did not believe what they faid." And fays he to me, " One day I was fitting in the houfe, and Egerly came in, and I fpake to him before the whole family (in the French tongue, for he could not fpeak much Englifh) and afked him

him of this ftory ; he anfwered, it is a great
falfehood, faying, he never appeared to me, nor
have I ever reported any fuch thing to any body ;
and that he had never been at mafs fince Zebediah's death." At the hearing of which, they
were filenced and put to fhame. We bleffed
God together, for difcovering their wickednefs,
and difappointing them in what they aimed at,
and prayed to God to deliver us and all the captives from delufions, and recover them who had
fallen, and fo parted. After which I took my
pen and wrote a letter to one Mr. Samuel Hill,
an Englifh captive, taken from Wells, who lived
at Quebec, and his brother Ebenezer Hill, to
make a difcovery of this lying plot, to warn them
of their danger, and affure them of the falfehood
of this report ; but the letter fell into the hands
of the priefts, and was never delivered. This
Egerly came home with us, fo that they gained
nothing but fhame by this ftratagem. God often
difappoints the crafty devices of wicked men.

In the latter end of fummer, they told me,
" they had news from New-England, by one
who had been a captive at Bofton, who faid that
the minifters at Bofton had told the French captives, that the Proteftant religion was the only
true religion ; and that as a confirmation of it,
they would raife a dead perfon to life before their
eyes, for their conviction ; and that having perfuaded one to feign himfelf dead, they came and
prayed over him, and then commanded him in
the name of Chrift, (whofe religion they kept
pure) to arife ; they called and commanded, but
he never arofe ; fo that inftead of raifing the
dead

dead, they killed the living ; which the bereaved
relations difcovered." I told them, " it was an
old lie and calumny againft Luther and Calvin,
new vamped, and that they only change the perfons and place ;" but they affirmed it to be a
truth : I told them, " I wondered they were fo
fond of a faith propagated, and then maintained
by lying words."

We were always out of hopes of being returned
before winter, the feafon proving fo cold in the
latter end of September, and were praying to God
to prepare our hearts, with an holy fubmiffion to
his holy will, to glorify his holy name in a way
of paffive obedience, in the winter. For my own
part, I was informed by feveral who came from
the city, that the lord intendant faid, if More
returned and brought word that Battis was in
prifon, he would put me into prifon, and lay me
in irons. They would not permit me to go into
the city, faying, I always did harm when I came
to the city, and if at any time I was at the city,
they would perfuade the governour to fend me
back again.

In the beginning of laft June, the fuperior of
the priefts came to the parifh where I was, and
told me, he faw I wanted my friend captain de
Beauville, and that I was ragged. But, fays he,
your obftinacy againft our religion difcourages
from providing better clothes. I told him, it
was better going in a ragged coat, than with a
ragged confcience.

In the beginning of laft June, went out an
army of five hundred Macquas and Indians, with
an intention to have fallen on fome Englifh towns
                                                        down

down Connecticut river ; but lighting on a Scata-
cook Indian, who afterwards ran away in the night,
they were difcouraged ; faying, he would alarm the
whole country.	About fifty, as fome fay, or
eighty, as others, returned.	Thus God reftrained
their wrath.

When they were promifing themfelves another
winter, to draw away the Englifh to popery, came
news that an Englifh brigantine was coming, and
that the honourable capt. Samuel Appleton efq.
was coming ambaffador, to fetch off the captives,
and capt. John Bonner with him.	I cannot tell
you how the clergy and others laboured to ftop
many of the prifoners.	To fome, lib ; to
others, money and yearly penfions, were offered,
if they would ftay.	Some they urged to tarry at
leaft till the fpring of the year, telling them, it
was fo late in the year, they would be loft by fhip-
wreck if they went now ; fome younger ones they
told, if they went home, they would be damned,
and burn in hell forever, to affright them.	Day
and night they were urging of them to ftay.
And I was threatened to be fent aboard, without
a permiffion to come afhore again, if I fhould
again difcourfe with any of the Englifh who were
turned to their religion.	At Montreal, efpecially,
all crafty endeavours were ufed to ftay the Englifh.
They told my child, if he would ftay, he fhould
have an honourable penfion from the king every
year ; and that his mafter, who was an old man,
and the richeft in Canada, would give him a great
deal ; telling him, if he returned he would be
poor, for (faid they) your father is poor, has loft
all his eftate, it was all burnt.	But he would not

H 2						be

be prevailed with to ſtay. Others were alſo in like manner urged to ſtay ; but God graciouſly brake the ſnare, and brought them out. They endeavoured, in the fall of the year, to prevail with my ſon to go to France, when they ſaw he would not come to their communion any more. One woman, belonging to the eaſtern parts, who had, by their perſuaſions, married an Engliſh captive, taken the laſt war, came away with her huſband, which made them ſay, they were ſorry they ever perſuaded her to turn to their religion, and then to marry : For inſtead of advancing their cauſe by it, they had weakened it ; for now they   not only loſt her, but another they thought they had made ſure of. Another woman, belonging to the Eaſtward, who had been flattered to their religion, to whom a bible was denied, till ſhe promiſed to embrace their religion, and then had the promiſe of it for a little time, opening her bible whilſt in the church, and preſent at maſs, ſhe read the fourth chapter of Deuteronomy, and received ſuch conviction whilſt reading, that before her firſt communion, ſhe fell off from them, and could never be prevailed with any more to be of their religion.

We have reaſon to bleſs God, who has wrought deliverance for ſo many, and yet to pray to God for a door of eſcape to be opened for the great number yet behind, not much ſhort of an hundred, many of whom are children, and of theſe not a few among the ſavages ; and having loſt the Engliſh tongue, will be loſt, and turn ſavages in a little time, unleſs ſomething extraordinary prevent.

The

The veſſel that came for us, in its voyage to Canada, ſtruck on a bar of ſands, and there lay in very great hazard for four tides ; and yet they ſaw reaſon to bleſs God for ſtriking there ; for had they got over that bar, they would at midnight, in a ſtorm of ſnow, have run upon a terrible ledge of rocks.

We came away from Quebec on October 25 ; and by contrary winds and a great ſtorm, we were retarded, and then driven back near the city, and had a great deliverance from ſhipwreck, the veſſel ſtriking twice on a rock in that ſtorm. But through God's goodneſs, we all arrived in ſafety at Boſton, November 21 ; the nu r of captives fifty-ſeven, two of whom were my children. I have yet a daughter of ten yeas of age, and many neighbours, whoſe caſe beſpeaks your compaſſion, and prayers to God to gather them, being out-caſts ready to periſh.

At our arrival at Boſton, we found the kindneſſes of the Lord in a wonderful manner, in God's opening the hearts of many, to bleſs God with us and for us, wonderfully to give for our ſupplies in our needy ſtate. We are under obligations to praiſe God, for diſpoſing the hearts of ſo many to ſo great charity, and under great bonds to pray for a bleſſing on the heads, hearts and families of them, who ſo liberally and plentifully gave for our relief. It is certain, that the charity of the whole country of Canada, though moved with the doctrine of merit, does not come up to the charity of Boſton alone, where notions of merit are rejected ; but acts of charity performed out of a right chriſtian ſpirit, from a ſpirit of
thankfulneſs

thankfulneſs to God, out of obedience to God's command, and unfeigned love and charity to them that are of the ſame family and houſehold of faith. The Lord grant, that all who deviſe ſuch liberal things, may find the accompliſhment of the promiſes made by God, in their own perſons, and theirs after them, from generation to generation.

I SHALL annex a ſhort account of the troubles beginning to ariſe in Canada. On May 16, arrived a canoe at Quebec, which brought letters from Miſſiſippi, written the May preceeding, giving an account that the plague was there ᵑd that one hundred and fifty French, in a very little e, had died of it; and that the ſavages, called the Léziłouways, were very turbulent, and had with their arrows wounded a jeſuit in five places, and killed a Frenchman that waited on him. In July, news came, that the nations up the river were engaged in a war one againſt the other, and that the French living ſo among them, and trading with them, were in great danger; that the Mitchel-macquinas had made war with the Mizianmies, and had killed a mendicant friar, and three other Frenchmen, and eleven ſavages, at a place called the ſtraits, where they are ſettling a garriſon and place for traffick; the Mitchel-macquinas had taken ſixteen Frenchmen priſoners, and burnt their trading houſes. Theſe tidings made the French very full of perplexing troubles; but the jeſuits are endeavouring to pacify them; but the troubles, when we came away, were rather encreaſing than leſſening; for the laſt letters from the French priſoners at Mitchel-macquina report, that the ſavages had ſent out two companies, one of an hundred and fifty, another of an hundred and ſixty, againſt the ſavages at the ſtraits; and they feared, they would engage as well againſt the French as the Indians.

THE END.

Reports·of DIVINE KINDNESS *; or,*
Remarkable Mercies should be faith-
fully published, for the Praise of GOD
the Giver ;

SET FORTH IN A

SERMON,

PREACHED AT BOSTON LECTURE, *December* 5, 1706.

BY JOHN WILLIAMS,

Pastor of the CHURCH of CHRIST in Deerfield,
soon after his Return from Captivity.

PSALM cvii. 13, 14, 15, 32. *He saved them out of their distresses. He brought them out of darkness, and the shadow of death ; and brake their bands in sunder. O that men would praise the Lord for his goodness ; and for his wonderful works to the children of men.—Let them exalt him also in the congregation of the people, and praise him in the assembly of the elders.*

PSALM xxxiv. 3. *O magnify the Lord with me, and let us exalt his name together.*

LUKE VIII. 39.

Return to thine own house, and shew how great things GOD *hath done unto thee.——*

THE infinitely wise disposer of all things, who aims at his own glory, in the governing of rational creatures, doth sometimes bring persons into the depths of distress ; and then magnify his power and grace in raising them up out of their afflictions : And in many respects, by such things, he has a design of advancing his own honour and glory in the world. We find in the context, a person in a very doleful, distressed condition : He seems to be forsaken of God, and made

made a poffeffion and dwelling place of evil fpirits, deprived of all human comforts and delights,
made to poffefs forrow and pain to fuch a degree,
as to be a common fubject or theme of difcourfe
for all men to relate doleful things about.   And
afterward, God, in very remarkable and wonderful works of power and mercy, not only gives
releafe from his forrowful poffeffion, but he is
fitting at the feet of Jefus, cloathed, and in his
right mind: Now this was done for the declarative and manifeftative glory and honour of God.
For when this man, for whom fuch great things
had be   done, petitions Chrift that he may abide
wit   1n, to hear from him, and pay his refpects
to him ; he receives commandment, to be glorifying the power and mercy of God, in declaring to
others what great things God had done for him.

1. A fubject of great mercy ; or a perfon
fpoken of, for whom God had done great things,
beftowed eminent mercies.

2. A particular and fpecial command from
Chrift, to be glorifying God in relating to others,
what mercies he had been the fubject of.

3. His obedience to the great command of Chrift.
He went and publifhed the great things done for
him by Chrift ; fo that from the command of Chrift,
and his obedience to it, for which he is commended, you may obferve this doctrinal conclufion.

Doct. It well becomes thofe who have had em-
    inent mercies, to be fhewing to others what
    great things God has done for them.

The holy fcriptures, in many places, confirm
this truth.   See Exod. xii. 25, 26, 27.   *And it
fhall*

shall come to pass, when ye be come to the land, which the Lord will give you, according as he hath promised, that ye shall keep this service. And it shall come to pass, when your children shall say unto you, what mean you by this service? That ye shall say, it is the sacrifice of the Lord's passover, who passed over the houses of the children of Israel in Egypt, when he smote the Egyptians, and delivered our houses. Exod. xiii. 8, 10. *And thou shalt shew thy son in that day, saying, this is done because of that which the Lord did unto me, when I came forth out of Egypt. Thou shalt therefore keep this ordinance in his season from year to year.* Psal. lxxviii. 3, 4. *Which we have heard and known, and our fathers have told us; we will not hide them from their children, shewing to the generation to come the praises of the Lord; and his strength, and his wonderful works that he hath done.* In the prosecution and handling of this truth, consider,

I. They who have had mercies, have had them from God. God is the bestower and giver of all our good things: All our mercies come to us by a divine providence, and ordering; not by casualty or accident: Neither are they of our own procuring and purchasing, or others, so as to exclude the providential disposing of God. It is God who returns the captivity of Zion, Psalm cxxvi. begin. *When the Lord turned again the captivity of Zion, we were like them that dream: Then was our mouth filled with laughter, and our tongue with singing. Then said they among the heathen, the Lord hath done great things for them. The Lord hath done great things for us; whereof we are glad: Turn again our captivity, O Lord.* The very heathen acknowledge

edge the good things bestowed upon, and done for the church, to be from God ; and God's own people acknowledge him for the mercies granted, and humbly supplicate mercies from him for the future. It is God who gathers the out-casts of Israel : It is he who takes away the captives of the mighty, the prey of the terrible ; who contends with them that contend with us, and saves our children. It is God who disperseth and gathers again : Therefore the psalmist, Psal. ciii. begin. calls upon his soul to bless the Lord, and not to forget all his benefits ; and saith, *It is God who forgiveth all thy iniquities, who healeth all thy diseases : Who redeemeth thy life from destruction, who crowneth thee with loving kindness and tender mercies,* &c. Sometimes God, in a more immediate and extraordinary way and manner, confers blessings and mercies ; sometimes in a more ordinary and mediate way ; but his providence is to be acknowledged in all : Not one single mercy comes to us, without a commission from that God by whom our very hairs are numbered.

II. It well becomes those who have had eminent mercies, to be showing to others what great things God hath done for them. Therefore you find the holy psalmist calling upon others, to give a listening ear, whilst he makes a narration of the salvations he had from God, Psal. lxvi. 16. *Come and hear, all you that fear God, and I will declare what he hath done for my soul.*

1*st Reason.* Because God aimed at the advancement of his own honour and glory, in the giving and dealing out of these mercies. God

makes

makes and difpofeth all things for his own honour
and glory. All works of providence are fome way
or other to advance the honour and glory of God in
the world. The glory of his power, wifdom,
mercy, juftice and holinefs, are fome way or
other advanced in a declarative and manifeftative
way and manner. Now it well becomes us to
fall in with the defign of God, and in an active
manner to be giving him glory. That God defigns to have glory given to him, is evident from
Pfal. l. 15. *And call upon me in the day of trouble,
I will deliver thee, and thou fhalt glorify me.* Exod.
vii. 5. *And the Egyptians fhall know that I am the
Lord, when I ftretch forth mine hand upon Egypt,
and bring out the children of Ifrael from among them.*
God has a defign to magnify his power, mercy
and covenant faithfulnefs, in the eyes of the world.

2d *Reafon.* Becaufe God has given us direct
precepts, and pofitive commands, in this way, to
be glorifying of him. God is our Lord and law-
giver, and he requires, that among other ways of
fhowing forth his praifes, we do it by rehearfing
his praife-worthy acts to the children of men :
So that in obedience to God, and anfwering that
high and noble end we were made for, it is requi-
fite that in this way we glorify God. It is
enough, that the great God, who hath taken us
into covenant relation to himfelf, has enjoined us
to fhew forth his praifes, in rehearfing to others
the falvations and favours we have been the fub-
jects of. The forementioned fcriptures, with
many others that might be enumerated, fuffi-
ciently demonftrate, that God calls for our thankful acknowledgments in this way ; and upon the

I

account

account of this being so agreeable to the revealed and perceptive will of God, the psalmist expresseth himself, as in Psal. cxlv. 4, 5, 6. *One generation shall praise thy works to another, and shall declare thy mighty acts. I will speak of the glorious honour of thy majesty, and of thy wondrous works. And men shall speak of the might of thy terrible acts : And I will declare thy greatness. They shall abundantly utter the memory of thy great goodness ; and shall sing of thy righteousness.* Verses 10, 11, 12. *All thy works shall praise thee, O Lord ; and thy saints shall bless thee. They shall speak of the glory of thy kingdom and talk of thy power : To make known to the sons of men his mighty acts, and the glorious majesty of his kingdom.*

3d *Reason.* Because hereby they will stir up others to bless God with them, and for them. A truly gracious soul finds by experience, that he can do but a little in glorifying God, and finds how far he falls short of the rule of duty in so reasonable a service as glorifying God. And being enlarged in desires that the glory due to God might be given him, doth call upon others to join with him in this heavenly service of praising God ; and therefore tells them what great things God has done. Psalm xxxiv. 2, 3, 4, 6. *My soul shall make her boast in the Lord : The humble shall hear thereof, and be glad. O magnify the Lord with me, and let us exalt his name together. I sought the Lord, and he heard me ; and delivered me from all my fears. This poor man cried, and the Lord heard him ; and saved him out of all his troubles.* When Moses told his father-in-law Jethro, the great things God had done for Israel, he glorifies

God

God on their behalf, Ex*od.* xviii. 8, &c. *And Moses told his father-in-law, all that the Lord had done unto Pharaoh, and to the Egyptians for Israel's sake, and all the travail that had come upon them by the way, and how the Lord delivered them. And Jethro rejoiced for all the goodness which the Lord had done to Israel; whom he had delivered out of the hand of the Egyptians. And Jethro said, blessed be the Lord, who hath delivered you out of the hand of the Egyptians, and out of the hand of Pharaoh, who hath delivered the people from under the hand of the Egyptians. Now I know that the Lord is greater than all gods: For in the thing wherein they dealt proudly, he was above them.* By this means, thanks will be given to God by many : As many have been praying to God for them, so many will be praising and blessing God with them and for them.

4th Reason. Because hereby they will often-times be advised and counselled how to improve such mercies to the glory of God. We are con-scious to ourselves of so much blindness, igno-rance, and darkness, that we cannot but own it a great thing to be in a way for the best counsel, what to do with our mercies, and what and how to return to God for them. Now the publish-ing the great things done by God for us, puts others in a capacity to be advising and telling us what temptations we may expect to meet with, and what will be needful on our part to avoid temptations, and how to over-come ; they will be counselling us, how to be in a way of render-ing to the Lord according to the benefits done unto us ; what duties God looks for the perform-ance of, and directions how to do duty. In a word,

word, we may be counselled how to order our whole conversation so as God may have glory, and our good purposes of honouring and glorifying God with our mercies, established. Prov. xx. 18. *Every purpose is established by counsel.* When Moses had told Jethro what great things God had done for Israel, he saith, Exod. xviii. 19. *Hearken now unto my voice, I wil give thee counsel, and God shall be with thee,* &c.

5th Reason. Because hereby they will be instrumental to put others upon trusting God, making him their hope and refuge in an evil day. Others will be excited to a seeking refuge under the shadow of his wings, Psal. xliv. begin. *We have heard with our ears, O God, our fathers have told us, what work thou didst in their days, in the times of old. How thou didst drive out the heathen,* &c. And then it is said, *Thou art my king, O God: Command deliverances for Jacob. Through thee will we push down our enemies: Through thy name will we tread them under that rise up against us. For I will not trust in my bow, neither shall my sword save me. In God we boast all the day long.* Others that have heard, will say, such and such an one was thus exercised, and God appeared for them, and put songs of praise to the Lord into their mouths ; we will commit our case to God too ; we will both hope and quietly wait for God's salvation too. Your telling others, how you have found God a prayer-hearing God, will encourage them, prayer-wise, to be committing their distressed and difficult cases to him. What an honour to be instrumental to any soul's comfort, and God's honour ; agreeable to this is

that

that Pſal. lxxviii. 5, 6, 7. *Which he commanded our fathers, that they ſhould make them known to their children: That the generation to come might know them, even the children which ſhould be born; who ſhould ariſe and declare them to their children: That they might ſet their hope in God, and not forget the works of God; but keep his commandments.*

6th Reaſon. Becauſe the works of God towards them, have been very wonderful. The pſalmiſt often ſpeaks of the works of God as marvellous; they are wonderful, if we conſider how God timed the mercy; when their feet well nigh ſlipt, when they could ſee no way of eſcape; as with the children of Iſrael at the Red ſea. How very wonderful and marvellous was the work of God, in putting by the wicked purpoſe of Haman againſt Mordecai and the Jews? If we conſider how God kept from falling, by making them paſs a right judgment on their ways and his ways, as Pſal. lxxiii. Yea, appearing to ſave them, when with Jonah they were ſaying, *They were caſt out of God's ſight.* All refuge ſeemed to fail, none ſhewing any care for their ſoul; even then God made good his word, on which he had cauſed them to hope, as Pſalm cxlii. *per totum.* The works of God are marvellous, if we conſider the way and manner of uſhering in the mercy, the inſtruments that were made uſe of, and how he diſappointed the counſels of the crafty.

7th Reaſon. Becauſe it is a good evidence, that they regarded and took notice of the works of God in mercy, and would not forget his wonderful works towards them. For hereby they put others under advantages to put them in mind what favours they have received from God.

I 2

Use I.

Use I. Of Instruction. And, First, It informs us, that it is very acceptable to God, for christians to entertain the report of the experiences of others, to excite their own hearts to glorify God. For if God make it a duty in the receiver to report, it lays the hearer under an obligation to set such remarks upon the passages of divine providence to others, as may be useful to engage their hearts to glorify God, for the favours and blessings he has bestowed upon others. And therefore, in obedience to God's command, that you may be under advantages to glorify God, I will now make a report of some of the great things God has done for those you have been putting up so many prayers to God for. God has eminently been fulfilling that word, Psalm cvi. 46. *He made them also to be pitied, of all those that carried them captives.*

God hath made those whose characters have been, that they were such whose tender mercies were cruelties ; such from whom one act of pity and compassion could scarce be expected, even such who have delighted in cruelty ; to pity and compassionate such who were led into captivity by them. Made them bear on their arms, and carry on their shoulders, our little ones, unable to travel. Feed their prisoners with the best of their provision : Yea, sometimes pinch themselves, as to their daily food, rather than their captives. To pity them under sickness, and afford all proper means for the restoration of their health, or recovery from lameness. Made heathen's bowels yearn towards poor infants exposed to death, so as to work out their deliverance from

fatal

fatal ftrokes, by burdening of themfelves. Oh !
let us adore the riches of the grace of God, who
in wrath remembers mercy, and doth not ftir up
all his wrath ; and from hence be encouraged,
when under convictions of God's being angry
with us, yet to look to him for mercy.

God has upheld many poor fouls under all
manner of difadvantages, as to getting of knowledge, and kept them from falling, though crafty
adverfaries were under all advantages, and painful
endeavours ufed to feduce them. Being without
bibles, minifters, or chriftian friends to confer
with, daily haraffed with temptations and temp-
ters : Some threatened, fome flattered, fome fhut
up and confined in monafteries, where no means
were uneffayed to gain them to change their
religion.

God has ftrengthened them to go through
tedious journeys, and renewed ftrength, when
they were even fainting in their fpirits ; thinking
it not poffible to travel five miles, and yet enabled
to travel at leaft forty in a day. Remarkably
ordering feafons, fo as to be for their comfort in
their travels ; caufing a moift fnow to fall on the
lake, only to fuch a height as to make it eafy to
their fwoln and wounded feet : Changing the
winds for their advantages, in petty voyages, in
their ticklifh canoes.

They have found God a little fanctuary to them,
in the land of ftrangers ; even there they have
found the confolations of God through Chrift not
to be fmall ; fo that fome of the moft joyful and
refrefhing favours from heaven, have been given
in to their fouls, when under all forts of outward
afflictions.   They

They have found God a God hearing prayers, when they have gone to him with their moſt difficult caſes, preſerving them from falling; re-covering theirs from fails; to making void the counſels of adverſaries, diſappointing them in the things they dealt moſt proudly in.   God has brought his to a reſignation to his will, and then appeared dealing out mercies, as the very caſe did require.

God has ſanctified to ſome, their former Sab-bath ſolemn attendances on duties of piety, pri-vate as well as publick; and a religious education to be an unanſwerable objection againſt ſuch who were zealous for the traditions of men, to a viſible profaning God's Sabbaths.   They durſt not em-brace that religion, whoſe principles as well as practices, were ſo contrary to the precepts of God's holy word.   Oh! how ſhould miniſters and parents be encouraged from hence to uſe their utmoſt care, that God's Sabbaths may be duly ſanctified by all under their charge; and that they would be exemplary before others, in a due obſervance of holy time.

God has made the falls of ſome to popery a means for the recovery of others; and making thoſe things, by which the adverſary thought to increaſe their numbers and proſelytes, to be oc-caſional of recovering ſuch who from their youth had been educated in the popiſh way; having been taken captives when young.   Do not be diſcouraged, and ſay, your friends and relations have (being captivated when young) for a long time lived in popery, and therefore no hopes of recovery; for God can make dry bones, very

dry,

dry, to live, and can in ways unthought of by you, both recover them after they have fallen, and return them again. The adverfaries have fometimes pretended miracles for the confirmation of their religion, that they might feduce to popery ; in fallacious ways caufed reports that fome captives died papifts ; that one appeared in flames of fire to bear a teftimony againft the Proteftant religion ; but God has, in his wife providence, made known their falfehoods and lies.

They have fought to perfuade fome, by fums of money, to change their religion, offering honour and advancement to them at the fame time ; but God has enabled them to refift and hate fuch allurements.

The reading the fourth chapter of Deuteronomy, a means of recovering one from popery.

God has made fome, with an heroical, yea with a right chriftian courage, to welcome death. Oh let every one get fuch a preparednefs for death, that a fudden death may not be a terror !

God has made fome, by the want of fanctuary mercies, to fet an higher value upon the ordinances of Jefus Chrift. Oh learn to prize and improve them, left God teach you, by the briars and thorns of the wildernefs, the worth of them, and make you weep when you fit down at the rivers of Babylon.

God has ftrengthened fome to ftand, when they have not only been threatened with all cruelties if they refufed, but when the hatchet has been lifted up, with a threatening of fpeedy death in cafe of refufal. Oh let every one truft in God, who is a feafonable help and a prefent refuge !

INSTRUCTION

INSTRUCTION II. How they are to blame, that do not regard and take notice of the works of God, nor treasure up the remembrance of them in their minds. How soon are mercies like to be forgotten ; the psalmist says, *Forget not all his benefits*. It was the great sin of the Israelites of old, that they soon forgat God's wonderous works. The holy God gave order, that his people should erect stones of remembrance, that his wonderful works of mercy to his people might not be forgotten ; yea, commanded parents to tell their children, from generation to generation, what great things he had done for them. How are they then to blame that say, *They bless God for their mercies*, and do not rehearse the praise-worthy works of divine providence to others.

USE II. To direct such, who have received great and eminent mercies from God, in this way of making known to others the wonders of mercy to them, to be praising God. It is one way very proper and agreeable to the revealed will of God : You must watch against all vain ostentation.

USE III. Of EXHORTATION. To all who have, in a more peculiar way and manner, been casting off the effects and fruits of divine bounty and goodness, to be declaring what great things God has done for them.

Therefore, 1. Beware of all manner of pride. Sometimes men cannot declare the great works of God done for them, without making known their own weakness, and therefore are silent, and hold their peace ; they had rather God should lose his glory, than they any of their credit or esteem.

efteem. But the holy pfalmift fays, *His feet had well nigh flipt ;* yea, *that in his hafte he had faid, all men are liars ;* and that one day he fhould furely perifh ; take fhame to himfelf, that he might magnify the preventing and delivering grace and goodnefs of God. Sometimes men's pride makes them fo admire their own parts and contrivances, as to over-look the works of divine providence ; they facrifice to their own net, and burn incenfe to their own drag ; and fay they have fo much learning and knowledge, that they could eafily anfwer arguments to feduce them to popery; and fo do not fee and acknowledge the goodnefs of God, in preferving and keeping them.

2. Beware of a ftupid, fenfelefs, flothful fpirit. The works of God are fought out of them that have pleafure in them. Some will not be at the pains to recollect the paffages of divine providence ; will not commit them to writing, or to their memories, and therefore foon forget them ; they never wifely obferve the heightening circumftances of their mercies.

Confider, 3. How heavenly an employ and fervice it is, to be glorifying and praifing God. It will be one part of the work of heaven, to be telling of the wonderful works of God towards us. Begin fuch an heavenly employ on earth. Hereby you will alfo intereft yourfelves in the prayers of others : To have many prayers going daily to God for you, how great a favour is it ! Others hearing what mercies you have had, will bear you upon their hearts when at the throne of grace, that you may fuitably improve fuch mercies.

The

The glorifying God is the greatest and chiefest concern of gracious souls ; and the glorifying of God here, is the way to be glorified by, and with God forever. The not glorifying God is very displeasing to him, and a way to deprive ourselves of the sweet and comfort of our mercies. God accounts forgetting of mercies, a forgetting himself.

END OF THE SERMON.

APPENDIX.

Drawn up and sent to the Rev. Mr. PRINCE, by the Rev. Mr. STEPHEN WILLIAMS, of Springfield, who on February 29th, 1703-4, was, with his Rev. father, Mr. JOHN WILLIAMS, of Deerfield, carried captive into Canada, but returned, and was educated at Harvard College.

Names of those Persons who were taken Captive at Deerfield, Feb. 29th, 1703-4.

MARY Alexander,
Mary Alexander, jun.
Joseph Alexander, *ran away the first night.*
Sarah Allen,
Mary Allis,
Thomas Baker,
Simon Beaumont,
Hannah Beaumont,
Hephzibah Belding,
John Bridgman, *ran away in the meadow.*
Nathaniel Brooks,
Mary Brooks,
Mary Brooks, jun.
William Brooks,
Abigail Brown,
Benjamin Burt,
John Burt,
Sarah Burt,
Hannah Carter,

Hannah Carter, jun.
Mercy Carter,
Samuel Carter,
John Carter,
Ebenezer Carter,
Marah Carter,
John Catlin,
Ruth Catlin,
Elizabeth Corse,
Elizabeth Corse, jun.
Daniel Crowfoot,
Abigail Denio,
Sarah Dickinson,
Joseph Eastman,
Mary Field,
John Field,
Mary Field, jun.
Mary Frary,
Thomas French,
Mary French,
Thomas French, jun.

Mary French, jun.
Freedom French,
Martha French,
Abigail French,
Mary Harris,
Samuel Hastings,
Elizabeth Hawks,
Mehuman Hinsdel,
Mary Hinsdel,
Jacob Hix, *died at Cowass.*
Deacon David Hoit, *died at Cowass.*
Abigail Hoit,
Jonathan Hoit,
Sarah Hoit,
Ebenezer Hoit,
Abigail Hoit, jun.
Elizabeth Hull,
Thomas Hurst,
Ebenezer Hurst,
Benoni Hurst,

Sarah Hurst,
Sarah Hurst, jun
Elizabeth Hurst,
† Hannah Hurst,
Martin Kellogg,
Martin Kellogg, jun.
Joseph Kellogg,
† Joanna Kellogg,
Rebecca Kellogg,
John Marsh,
Sarah Multoon,
* Philip Multoon,
* Frank, a negro.
* Mehitable Nims,
Ebenezer Nims,
† Abigail Nims,
Joseph Petty,
Sarah Petty,

Lydia Pomroy,
Joshua Pomroy,
Esther Pomroy,
Samuel Price,
† Jemima Richards,
† Josiah Riseing,
Hannah Shelden,
Ebenezer Shelden,
Remembrance Shelden,
Mary Shelden,
John Stebbins,
Dorothy Stebbins,
John Stebbins, jun.
Samuel Stebbins,
† Ebenezer Stebbins,
† Joseph Stebbins,
† Thankful Stebbins,
† Elizabeth Stevens,

Ebenezer Warner,
* Waitstill Warner,
† Waitstill Warner, jun.
Sarah Warner,
Rev. John Williams,
* Mrs. Eunice Williams,
Samuel Williams,
Stephen Williams,
† Eunice Williams, jun.
Esther Williams,
Warham Williams,
John Weston,
Judah Wright.

Three Frenchmen who
had lived in the town for
some time, and came from
Canada, were also taken.

NOTE. Where there is this sign * against the person's name, it is to signify they were killed after they went out of town : And this mark † is
to signify that they are still absent from their native country.

Names of those who were slain at that time in or near the town.

SLAIN IN THE TOWN.

DAVID Alexander,
Thomas Carter,
John Catlin,
Jonathan Catlin,
Sarah Field,
Samson Frary,
John French,
Alice Hawks,
John Hawks, jun. and
his wife,
Thankful Hawks,
John Hawks,
Martha Hawks,

Samuel Hinsdale,
Joseph Ingersol,
Jonathan Kellogg,
Philip Matloon's wife
and child,
Parthena, a negro.
Henry Nims,
Mary Nims, *
Mercy Nims,
Mehitable Nims,
Sarah Price,
Mercy Root,
Thomas Shelden,

Mrs. Shelden,
Mercy Shelden,
Samuel Smead's wife and
two children,
Elizabeth Smead,
Martin Smith,
Serg. Benoni Stebbins,
Andrew Stevens,
Mary Wells,
John Williams, jun.
Jerusha Williams.

SLAIN IN THE MEADOW.

SAMUEL Allis,
Serg. Boltwood,
Robert Boltwood,

Joseph Catlin,
Samuel Foot,
David Hoit, jun.

Jonathan Ingram,
Serg. Benjamin Wait
Nathaniel Warner.

* These three it was supposed were burnt in the cellar.

---

*An account of the mischief done by the enemy in Deerfield, from
beginning of its settlement to the death of the Rev Mr.
JOHN WILLIAMS, in June, 1729.*

THE enemy beset the place, and killed one
Egleston, September 1, 1675.

The Indians fell upon the people as they were going
back worship, on Sept. 12. 1675, and wounded one
Harrington in the neck, but the wound did not
K   prove

prove mortal. One man was drove into the swamp, taken and killed.

3. Captain Lothrop and company were slain at Muddy brook (alias) Bloody brook, on Sept. 18, 1675.

4. The *fall fight* (as it is called) was on May 18, 1676, when a great slaughter was made of the enemy, but Capt. Turner and 37 men were lost. There were many remarkables, relating to this affair, (as related by Jonathan Wells, Esq. who was present) which are not taken notice of by Mr. Hubbard, or Dr. Mather.

5. Sept. 19, 1677. John Root was killed, and Serg. Plympton, Quintin Stockwell, and Benoni Stebbins, were taken captive, but Stebbins made his escape from them and got home. This was after they began to settle the place a second time ; for upon capt. Lothrop's loss, the town was deserted for some time ; but this year, 1677, they began to build again. Serg. Plympton was accounted a gracious man ; he was burnt by the Indians, and the Indians obliged one Dickinson, taken at Hatfield, to lead him to the stake : The manner of burning was this ; they covered him with dry bark, set it on fire, then they quenched the fire, and anon firing it again. He went cheefully to the stake, &c. The town was deserted for some time : In 1684, they returned again to settle the town.

6. June, 1693. The widow Hepzibah Wells and her three daughters were knocked on the head and scalped, two of them died, but the other lived ; at the same time Thomas Broughton was killed, and his wife, great with child, and three of their children.

7. On October 13, 1693. Martin Smith was taken, and carried to Canada, from whence he returned after some years.

8. Sept. 15, 1694. Monsieur Castreen, with a number of Indians, beset the fort, but were beat off : Daniel Severance (a lad) was killed in the meadow ; and John Beaumont, and Richard Lyman, soldiers in the fort, were wounded, but recovered. Mrs. Hannah Beaumont and some children who were her scholars, were remarkably preserved : As they ran from the house to the fort, the enemy fired many shot at them, and the bullets whistled about their ears ; but none of them were hurt, although some of the enemy were very near them.

9. August 18, 1695. Mr. Joseph Barnard was fired upon by the enemy, and his horse was shot down : He himsel

himself was wounded in the body, one wrist shivered to pieces, his other hand wounded ; but yet through the bravery of Godfry Nims, and others with him, he was brought into the town, and lived till Sept. 6, and then died, greatly lamented, &c.

10. Sept. 16, 1696. John Gillet and John Smead, were hunting up green river ; the Indians came upon them, and took Gillet, but Smead made his escape ; the enemy left two or three men with Gillet, and the rest came along to the town, and assaulted Daniel Belding's house, took Mr. Belding, his son Nathaniel, and daughter Esther, captive : Killed his wife and three children, and wounded Samuel and Abigail, but they recovered, although Samuel had a hatchet stuck in his head, and some of his brains came out at the wound.

11. July, 1698. Nathaniel Pomroy was killed, being with a party of men that went up the river after some Indians that had done mischief at Hatfield : At the same time Samuel Dickinson, and one ——— Charly, were retaken from the enemy. This is related by Dr. Cotton Mather, in his history of the ten years war, &c.

12. October 8, 1703. Zebediah Williams and John Nims, were taken captive, and carried to Canada ; Williams died there ; Nims, with some others, made their escape, and got home to Deerfield, in 1705.

13. The town was taken February 29, 1703.

14. May 11, 1704. John Allen and his wife were killed at a place called the Barrs.

15. Serg. John Hawks, riding on the road, was fired at by the enemy, and wounded in the hand, but got off to Hatfield, and his wound was healed, &c. This was in the summer of 1704.

16. July 19, 1704. Thomas Russell was killed by the enemy, north of the town.

17. August, 1708. A scout went up to the white river, and as they returned, were fired upon by the enemy, and one man, whose name was Barber, was killed ; and he killed the Indian that killed him. Martin Kellogg, jun. was taken captive, and the rest escaped.

18. Oct. 26, 1708. E. Field was killed near muddy brook.

19. Mehuman Hinsdale was taken captive as he was driving his team from Northampton. This was April 11, 1709 : The second time of his captivity : He was carried

to Canada, and from thence to France, and got to England, and from thence home, &c.

20. May, 1709. Lieut. John Wells, and John Burt, were loſt in a ſkirmiſh with the enemy on the French river, after they had been, with others, as far as Lake Champlain, and killed ſome of the enemy.

21. Joſeph Cleſſon and John Arms were taken June 22, 1709, and the next day Jonathan Williams was killed, and Matthew Cleſſon mortally wounded ; and lieut. Thomas Taylor and Iſaac Matloon were wounded, but recovered.

22. July 30, 1712. *Serg. Samuel Taylor, and others, were ſent out as a ſcout to the north river, they were attacked by the enemy, and Samuel Androſs was killed ; Jonathan Barrett was wounded in the ſide, and then taken ; one William Sandford was alſo taken, the reſt got home, &c. The priſoners were carried to Canada, where they met lieut. Samuel Williams, (who was then at Canada with a flag of truce), who ranſomed them from the Indians, and brought them home : They were abſent but about two months.

23. June 27, 1724. Ebenezer Shelden, Thomas Colton, and Jeremiah Engliſh, (a friend Indian), were killed on the road beyond the green river houſes ; and it was ſuppoſed the enemy received ſome damage from ſome of our forces, who came upon them ſpeedily, &c.

24. July 10, 1724. Lieut. Timothy Childs and Samuel Allen, were ſhot upon and wounded, as they were returning from their labour in the field, but they eſcaped, and were healed of their wounds.

25. Auguſt 25, 1725. Deacon Field, deacon Childs, and others, were going up to green river farms, and were ambuſhed by the Indians, but they diſcovered the Indians ; and John Wells diſcharged his gun at an Indian, who fell : The Indians fired at them, and wounded deacon Samuel Field, the ball paſſing through the right hypocondria, cutting off three plaits of the myſenteria, which hung out of the wound, in length almoſt two inches, which was cut off even with the body, the bullet paſſing between the loweſt and the next rib, cutting, at its going forth, the loweſt rib : His hand being cloſe to the body when the ball came forth, it entered at the root of the heel of the thumb, cutting the bone of the fore finger, and, reſting between the fore and ſecond finger, was cut out, and all the wounds were cured in leſs than five weeks, by doctor Thomas Haſtings,

APPENDIX.

By the Rev. John Taylor, *the present minister of the Gospel, in Deerfield ; containing some account of the mischief done by the enemy, in Deerfield, and its vicinity, from the death of the* Rev. Mr. Williams, *to the conclusion of the last French war.*

THE readers of this appendix, will probably feel desirous of knowing the reasons, why, in many things, I have been so general ; only having given a brief statement of facts ; and in others, have been more particular. I trust, it will be a sufficient apology to observe, that I have done it for want of better documents. Most of the facts mentioned, I have taken from the minutes of some gentlemen, who kept them, only for their own satisfaction, and were not particular ; and now, the distance of time, precludes the possibility of obtaining such an account of circumstances, as may be depended on.

One reason, of my adding this appendix, is, I suppose that it will not be disagreeable to any who were desirous that the narrative should be reprinted, especially the descendants of those who were either killed, wounded, or captivated ; and for this reason I have been careful also to mention the names of such.

Another reason is, I think that every vestige of history, which respects the early settlement of a country, should be preserved, for the satisfaction of future generations.

THE last account of mischief, mentioned in the former appendix, done by the enemy in this part of the country, was in August, 1725. This year, terminated the war. A treaty of peace was held at Boston, by commissioners from the General Court, and the chiefs of the Indian tribes ; at which, articles were signed, and a long peace ensued.

There appeared, for many years, an unusually pacific spirit among the Indians ; probably in consequence of some acts of the General Court, favourable to them in their trade. It was thought, that they never again would have been disposed to hostilities, had they not been under the immediate influence of French interest.

War was declared between France and England, March, 1744. The first year of the war, no Indians made their

K 2 appearance

appearance in this part of the country : They had found
by experience, that to maintain an open trade with the
English, was greatly for their interest ; and consequently
at first, entered into the war with reluctance.

The first mischief that I can obtain an account of, done
by the enemy, in this part of the country, in the course of
this war, was in July, 1745 ; when a few Indians came to
a place called the great meadow, about 16 miles above fort
Dummer, on Connecticut river ; two of whom, captivated
William Phips, as he was hoeing his corn. After having
taken, and led him about half a mile, they made a stand ;
and as the Indians afterwards informed, one of them having laid down his gun, and gone a few rods, for the purpose of fetching something he had left, on his return, Phips
took up the Indian's gun, fired upon, and killed him ;
then fell upon the other with his hoe, struck him down,
and bruised him, until he supposed he was dead ; he then
attempted to make his escape, but unfortunately, three
more of the enemy came upon him, and killed him.

The same month, deacon Josiah Fisher, was killed, and
scalped at a place called the upper Ashwelot.

October 11. The fort at the great meadow, was attacked by a large party of French and Indians ; the attack was
bold, and furious, but without success. No lives were lost.
Nehemiah Howe was taken captive, and carried to Quebec,
where he soon died. The enemy on their return, met one
David Rugg, with another person, passing down Connecticut river in a canoe ; Rugg they killed, and scalped, the
other person, with some difficulty, made his escape.

I can find no farther account of mischief done by the
enemy, in this part of the country, in the year 1745, but
in 46 they began in season, and the sufferings of the people
were very considerable.

In April, the enemy made their appearance at No. 4,
(now Charleston), which was then the most northern settlement, on Connecticut river ; capt. John Spafford, Isaac
Parker, and Stephen Farnsworth, being at a little distance
from the fort, were captivated, and carried to Canada.

The same month, a party of Indians ambushed the road, between Northfield and Lunenburgh, and killed Joshua Holton.

On the 23d of the same month, a large party of the
enemy, came to the upper Ashwelot, with a design to have
taken the fort by surprise, but being discovered by a person
who

who was providentially at that time at a little distance from the garrison, they were disconcerted; an action however ensued, which continued for some time; the enemy finally withdrew. In this action, John Bullard was killed, Nathan Blake was captivated, and the wife of Daniel M'Kinne, being out of the fort, was overtaken and stabbed. Before the enemy retired, they burnt several buildings, which was supposed to have been done, not so much for the sake of mischief, as to conceal their dead; there being many human bones afterwards found among the ashes.

In the beginning of May, the enemy again appeared at No. 4; a few people were near a barn, about sixty rods from the fort, when they were fired upon by a considerable body who had concealed themselves in the barn. Seth Putnam, a soldier belonging to the fort, was killed; whilst the enemy were endeavouring to scalp him, major Willard, commander of the garrison, with two soldiers, ran near to them undiscovered, and fired upon them, upon which they retreated with great haste. The Indians afterwards reported to the prisoners in Canada, that at this time two of their number were mortally wounded, and died soon after.

May 6, a large party of Indians made an attempt upon the fort at Falltown; (now Bernardston), a person about forty rods from the fort discovering them, gave information to another farther distant than himself; by this the enemy found they were discovered, and ran immediately to the fort; an attack commenced, which continued for some time, and though there were but three soldiers in the fort, they defended it till the enemy withdrew. John Burk was slightly wounded, one house was burnt, and about ten cattle were killed. Two Indians were mortally wounded, who died soon after their return.

On the same day, Serg. John Hawks, and John Miles, were fired upon by two Indians, as they were riding out from fort Massachusetts, and were both wounded: Miles made his escape to the fort; Hawks fought for some time, and as afterwards appeared, might have taken them both prisoners had he understood their language; they asked him for quarter before he turned to make his escape.

10th. Five of that party of Indians, who the day before had been at Falltown fort, ambushed the road at Colrain. Matthew Clark, with his wife and daughter, together with two soldiers were fired upon, a few rods from the fort;

Clark

Clark was killed, and his wife and daughter were wounded; one of the foldiers returning the fire, killed one of the enemy, which gave them a check, and he brought the wounded into the fort.

A few days after, about twenty men were out, fifty or fixty rods from the fort, at No. 4, viewing the place where Parker was killed on the 2d of the month, and before they difcovered an enemy, they were fired upon by a large body of Indians, who immediately endeavoured to cut off their communication with the fort; capt. Stevens, commander of the garrifon, came out with a body of men for their relief, a fevere action commenced, which continued for fome time; at laft the enemy fled; and as was fuppofed with confiderable lofs. Capt. Stevens loft three, viz. Aaron Lyon, Peter Perrin, and Jofeph Marcy; he had four wounded, and one taken captive.

June 11. A party of the enemy again appeared at fort Maffachufetts; a number of men being at fome diftance from the fort, were attacked, and a fkirmifh enfued: The enemy fled, after fuftaining the fire but a few moments. Elifha Nims, and Gerfhom Hawks were wounded; and Benj. Tenter was captivated. One of the enemy was killed.

19th. A large body of the enemy again appeared at No. 4; capt. Stevens, and capt. Brown, marching with about fifty men from the fort into the meadow, were ambufhed; the enemy were difcovered before they fired: Stevens began the attack, and a fevere action enfued; after fome time the enemy were repulfed, and retreated in great hafte and confufion. Capt. Stevens loft none on the fpot. Jedediah Winchel was mortally wounded, and died foon after. David Parker, Jonathan Stanhope, and Noah Heaton were alfo wounded, but recovered.

20th. A party of about twenty Indians came to Bridgman's fort, about two miles below fort Dummer, and fell upon a number of men who were at work in the meadow. In this fkirmifh William Robins and James Parker were killed; John Beaumont and Daniel How were taken captive; M. Gilfon, and Patrick Ray were wounded, but recovered.

July 3. The enemy waylaid a mill in Hinfdale; colonel Willard having come to the mill with a guard of about 20 men, for the purpofe of grinding, and having placed his guards, they were foon fired upon; the col. calling to his men with great earneftnefs to fall upon them, gave them

fuch

such a fright, that they fled, leaving behind them their packs, and provisions, to the value of 40ˡ. old tenor.

28th. David Morrison, of Colrain, was taken captive, near one of the garrisons.

August 3. A body of the enemy appeared at No. 4 ; suspicions of their approach were excited by the yelling of dogs. A scout was sent out from the fort, and had proceeded but a few rods before they were fired on. Ebenezer Philips was killed ; the remainder made their escape to the fort ; the enemy surrounded the garrison, and endeavoured, for three days, to take it ; but finding their efforts ineffectual, they withdrew, after having burnt several buildings, and killed all the cattle, horses, &c. which they could find.

11th. Benj. Wright, of Northfield, riding in the woods, was fired on, and mortally wounded ; he died in a few hours.

17th. Ezekiel Wallingford was killed, and scalped, at a place called Poquiag. The same day, a person by the name of Bliss, was killed, and scalped, on the road between Deerfield, and Colrain, or Bernardston.

20th An army of about nine hundred French and Indians, under command of gen. de Vaudreuil, made an attack upon fort Massachusetts. The fort was commanded by col. Hawks, who, unfortunately, was not in a situation to defend it against such a force, having but thirty-three persons, men, women, and children, in the fort ; and being miserably provided with ammunition ; with great fortitude, he defended it for twenty eight hours ; and had not his ammunition failed, it is probable he never would have given up the fort. He was, finally, necessitated to capitulate ; and he offered such articles as were accepted by de Vaudreuil. One special article in this capitulation, was, that none of the prisoners should be delivered into the hands of the Indians ; the next day, however, Vaudreuil divided the prisoners, and delivered them one half, in open violation, and contempt of the article. * The Indians immediately killed one, who, by reason of sickness, was unable to travel. The prisoners were, in general, treated with civility, most of whom were afterwards redeemed. Col. Hawks lost but one man in the siege. Gen. de Vaudreuil, according to the best

---

* General de Vaudreuil's plea for this breach of faith, was, the danger of mutiny in his army, the Indians being irritated to a great degree, on account of their being cut off, by the capitulation, from all the profits of the conquest. But, how far this plea was a justification of such perfidy, I leave to the judicious to determine.

beſt accounts the priſoners could obtain, loſt forty-five, who
were either killed outright, or died of their wounds.

Immediately after the capture of the fort, a party of
about fifty Indians came on, for the purpoſe of making de-
predations upon Deerfield. They came firſt upon a hill, at
the ſouth weſt corner of the ſouth meadow, where they diſcovered ten, or twelve, men and children at work, in a ſitu-
ation, in which they might all, with eaſe, be made priſoners.
Had they ſucceeded in their deſign, which was, to obtain
priſoners, rather than ſcalps, it is probable that events would
not have been ſo diſaſterous as they proved. They were
diſconcerted by the following circumſtance : Mr. Eleazer
Hawks was out that morning a fowling, and was providentially at the foot of the hill, at the time the enemy came
down ; they, ſeeing him, ſuppoſed they were diſcovered;
and immediately fired upon him, killed, and ſcalped him.
This gave an alarm to the people in the meadow, ſome of
whom were but a few rods diſtant. The enemy were now
ſenfible, that what they did muſt be done with diſpatch.
Accordingly they ruſhed into the meadow, fired on Simeon
Amſden, a lad, and killed him, beheaded, and ſcalped him.
Mr. Samuel Allen, John Sadler, and Adonijah Gillet, ran
a few rods, and made a ſtand, under the bank of the river,
where they were attacked with fury, and fought for a little
time with great bravery ; they were, however, ſoon over-
powered with numbers. Allen and Gillet fell. Sadler,
finding himſelf alone, ran acroſs the river, and made his
eſcape, amidſt a ſhower of balls. Whilſt this was paſſing,
Oliver Amſden was purſued a few rods, overtaken, and
ſtabbed, after having his hands and fingers cut in pieces, by
endeavouring to defend himſelf againſt the enemies' knives.
At the ſame time, three children by the name of Allen, all
of whom are ſtill living, were purſued ; Eunice, one of the
three, was ſtruck down with a tomahawk, which was ſunk
into her head, but by reaſon of the haſte in which the enemy
retreated, ſhe was left unſcalped, and afterwards recovered.
Caleb, the preſent Mr. Caleb Allen, of Deerfield, made his
eſcape ; and Samuel was taken captive, the only priſoner
who was taken at this time.* The firing immediately
alarmed

* This lad, after a year and nine months, was redeemed. Col. Hawks,
who was ſent to Canada for the purpoſe of redeeming captives, after en-
quiring for the lad, was informed, that he was unwilling to be ſeen, and
that he expreſſed great diſſatisfaction upon hearing of his arrival : When
he

alarmed the town.   Capt. Hopkins, commander of the
standing guard, together with most of the inhabitants, as
volunteers, came on with the utmost expedition, but the
enemy had withdrawn in great haste, expecting, no doubt,
a violent attack ; they were pursued several miles by a
body of men, under the command of capt. Cleffon, but
could not be overtaken.

It does not appear, as a matter of certainty, that more
than one of the enemy was killed at this time, and him, by
Samuel Allen ; sometime after, however, the remains of a
person were found, near the place of action, supposed to be
those of an Indian.

This was the last mischief, done by the enemy, in the
western frontiers, this season.

April 7, 1747.   A large body of French, and Indians,
appeared at No. 4, and laid siege to the garrison, which
continued for three days, when the enemy withdrew, having done but little damage ; only slightly wounding Joseph
Ely, and John Brown.

15th.   Nathaniel Dickinson, and Asahel Burt, of Northfield, being out a little distance from the town, were killed,
and scalped.   The enemy, on their return from Northfield,
burnt most of the buildings in Winchester, and in the upper, and lower Ashwelots, which plantations, a few days
before, had been deserted by the inhabitants, not having
sufficient protection afforded them by government.

May 25.   As fort Massachusetts was rebuilding, there
being several hundred people present, an army of the enemy
came, with a design to hinder the undertaking.   About an
hundred men, a few days before, had been sent to Albany,
for stores of provisions, and ammunition ; being on their
return, and near the fort, a scout was sent forward, who,
coming within sight of the fort, discovered the enemy, and
began an attack ; this gave an alarm to the people at the
fort,

he was brought into the presence of col. Hawks, he was unwilling to know
him, although he was his uncle, and had always been acquainted with him
in Deerfield ; neither would he speak in the English tongue, not that he
had forgotten it, but to express his unwillingness to return ; he made use
of various arts, that he might not be exchanged ; and finally could not be
obtained but by threats, and was brought off by force.   In this we see the
surprising power of habit ; this youth had lost his affection for his country,
and his friends, in the course of one year, and nine months ; and had be-
come so attached to the Indians, and their mode of living, as that to this
day, he considers that of the Indians, the happiest life.   This appears
more surprising when we consider, that he fared extremely hard, and was
reduced almost to a skeleton.

fort, who, as yet, had not discovered the enemy ; a few issued out, and maintained a small skirmish, till the enemy withdrew. There was, at the time, much complaint, both of the people at the fort, and of the commander of that party who was with the waggons, for not affording assistance, which was imputed to cowardice. In this action, three persons were wounded ; and a friend Indian, who belonged to Stockbridge, was killed.

July 15. Eliakim Sheldon, of Bernardston, was fired upon, and wounded ; he died the following night.

The same month, John Mills, of Colrain, passing from what was called the south fort, to his own house, was fired upon and killed.

August 26. A small party of the enemy came to a village belonging to Northampton, (now Southampton), and killed, and scalped, Elijah Clark, as he was threshing in his barn.

October 1. Peter Burvee was taken captive near Massachusetts' fort.

19th. John Smead, as he was travelling from Northfield to Sunderland, was killed, and scalped, near the mouth of Miller's river. He had but a few days before returned from captivity, being one who was taken at Massachusetts' fort, with his wife, and children.

About this time, Jonathan Sawtel was taken captive, from Hinsdale.

14th. As twelve men were passing down the river, from No. 4, they were ambushed, and a skirmish ensued ; Nathaniel Gould, and Thomas Goodall, were killed, and scalped ; Oliver Avery was wounded, and John Henderson taken captive, the remainder made their escape.

March 15, 1748. About eight men were out a few rods from the fort, at No. 4, and were attacked by about twenty Indians, who endeavoured to cut off their retreat to the fort ; a skirmish ensued, in which Charles Stevens was killed ; a man by the name of Androus was wounded, and Eleazer Priest was taken captive.

April 12. Jason Babcock was taken prisoner, being at work in his field, at Poqniag.

May 9. Noah Pixley was killed, and scalped, at Southampton.

About the same time, capt. Melvin, with eighteen men, being at the lake, near Crownpoint, fired at two canoes of Indians : On his return, being on West river, about 35
miles

miles from fort Dummer, was ambushed, and being fired on by surprise, his men were scattered: Two or three returned the fire, and killed two of the enemy: The same persons, after having gone some distance, and having fallen in company with three or four of their own men, concluded to return back, and give the enemy a shot; on their return they were fired on, and one was killed; they returned the fire, and killed one of the enemy. The whole company, excepting six, made their escape through the woods, and came in at different times. In this skirmish, Joseph Petty, John Heywood, John Dod, Daniel Mann, and Isaac Taylor, were killed; Samuel Severance could not be found, and was supposed to be taken captive. The loss of these men, was much lamented; and they are spoken of with respect, as prudent, virtuous men, and resolute soldiers.

June 16. As thirteen men were marching from colonel Hinsdale's, to fort Dummer, they were ambushed by a large body of the enemy and were fired upon. Joseph Richardson, Nathan French, and John Frost, were killed the first shot, and seven were immediately taken captive, viz. Henry Stevens, Benjamin Osgood, William Blanchard, Matthew Wiman, Joel Johnson, Moses Perkins, and William Bickford. Bickford was either killed by the enemy, the first night, or had been wounded, and died of his wounds.

26th. Capt. Hobbs, passing through the woods from No. 4, to fort Shirley, with forty men, and being about twelve miles northwest of fort Dummer, was attacked by a large body of the enemy, who had pursued him; it being in the middle of the day, he had made a stand, that his men might receive some refreshment; whilst they were dining, the scout, which was sent upon the back track, were fired on. Upon this, capt. Hobbs put his men into as much readiness for an action, as two or three minutes would admit of. The enemy came on with great fury, expecting, no doubt, an immediate surrendry; but capt. Hobbs gave them a warm reception, and fought, for four hours, with such boldness and fortitude, as that had he, and his men, been Romans, they would have received a laurel, and their names would have been handed down with honour, to the latest posterity; the enemy finally fled in haste, and with great loss. Capt. Hobbs, in this action, lost but three men, and had but three wounded; those killed were Ebenezer Mitchel, Eli Scott, and Samuel Gunn.

I.

July 14. As a scout of seventeen men were passing from col. Hinsdale's to fort Dummer, they were ambushed, and fired upon, by about 120 of the enemy ; two only were killed the first shot ; two more were wounded, and but four made their escape ; the remainder were taken captive ; the wounded the enemy killed, after having carried them about a mile.

23d. The enemy waylaid the main street, at Northfield, and killed Aaron Belding.

August 2. About 200 of the enemy, made their appearance at fort Massachusetts ; the fort was then under the command of capt. Ephraim Williams : A scout was first fired upon, which drew out capt. Williams, with about thirty men ; an attack began, which continued for some time ; but, finding the enemy numerous, capt. Williams fought upon the retreat, till he had again recovered the fort : The enemy soon withdrew, and with what loss was unknown. In this action, one Abbot was killed, lieut. Hawley, and Ezekiel Wells were wounded, but recovered.

This is the last account I can find, of mischief done by the enemy in the western frontiers, in what is called the first French war. Peace, however, was not finally settled with the Indians, until October 1749, when a treaty was held at Falmouth, by commissioners from the General Court, and the chiefs of the Indian tribes, by whom a former treaty, with some additions, was renewed.

Peace between France and England, took place in the year 1748, and war was again declared in 1756 ; but, in the summer of 55, a body of Indians appeared at Stockbridge, killed several persons, and did considerable mischief, in killing cattle, &c.

In June, the same summer, a number of persons being at work in the meadow, at the upper part of Charlemont, were fired on by a party of the enemy ; not so much mischief was done, as might have been expected ; a number made their escape : Cap. Rice, and Phinehas Arms, were killed, their bodies were afterwards found in a mangled condition. Titus King, and a lad, were taken captive.

The same month, capt. Bridgman's fort, at Hinsdale, was taken by stratagem, and a number of persons were captivated. It was supposed that the enemy had been lurking about for some time, and the situation of the fort was such as that whatever passed, either in, or near it,
might

might be eafily feen from the hills a little back : It was
the cuftom of the fort, for the women within to faften the
gate when the men went into the fields to labour, and to
open it upon their return, from the fignai of knocking :
The Indians obferving this, took an opportunity when the
men were at the greateft diftance from the fort, came, and
knocked at the gate ; and the women, being under no
fpecial apprehenfions of an enemy, immediately threw open
the gate, when, to their aftonifhment, they found the enemy entering ; no refiftance was made in the fort, and
fourteen perfons were taken captive. The enemy made no
longer tarry at the fort, than to fecure the prifoners, but
rufhed into the meadow, and fell upon the men, who, as yet,
had not difcovered what had paffed at the fort ; they made as
much refiftance as their fituation would admit of. In this fkirmifh, C. Howe was killed, the remainder made their efcape.

About this time, the fort at Keene, under the command
of capt. Sims, was attacked by a large party of Indians,
and with great fury ; the attack was lengthy, but was fuftained with fortitude. The enemy finding their attempts
to take the fort ineffectual, gave over the attack, but
wreaked their vengeance on the inhabitants, by deftroying
all the property they could find, in killing cattle, burning
buildings, &c. In this fiege, no lives were loft, and but one
perfon was taken captive, he being out of the fort at the time.

July 3. The enemy appeared at Keene, and captivated
a perfon by the name of Frizzle.

The fame month, fort Hinfdale was attacked by a confiderable body of the enemy. In this attack two perfons
were killed, and one was taken captive ; one of the
perfons killed was John Alexander.

About the fame time, two men were killed, at Bellows's
fort. Alfo, a man, by the name of Pike, was killed at
fome place up the river, but where I cannot tell.

June 7, 1756. Jofiah Fofter, with his family, were
taken captive, at Winchefter. The fame day, a body of
the enemy appeared at fort Maffachufetts. Benjamin
King, and a man by the name of Meacham, were killed.

The fame month, lieut. Jofeph Willard, was killed at No. 4.

On the 25th, as a number of men were coming from the
army at the lake, they were attacked by a large body of
the enemy, and it is probable that a fevere action enfued,
tho' I cannot afcertain the particulars ; there were, however,
eight men killed, and five taken captive.   July

July 11. The enemy came to Weft Hoofick, and killed capt. Chapin, and two perfons by the name of Chidefter.

Auguft 12, 1756. A party of five, or fix Indians, made their appearance in Deerfield, (now Greenfield), at a place called the country farms ; feveral men, viz. Benjamin Haftings, John Graves, Daniel Graves, Nathaniel Brooks, and Shubal Atherton, being at work, were furprifed, by difcovering the enemy between them and their guns, and being in no fituation to make any refiftance, found no way to fave themfelves, but by flight. They had fled but a few rods, before they were fired on ; none were either killed, or wounded the firft fhot ; the enemy ftill purfued, and continued their firing. Shubal Atherton was foon killed ; Benjamin Haftings, and John Graves, made their efcape ; Daniel Graves, and Nathaniel Brooks, were taken captive. Graves was killed, after the enemy had conveyed him but a little diftance ; he was in years, and it was fuppofed, he was unable to travel with fuch fpeed as the enemy wifhed. Brooks never returned from his captivity.

1757. The enemy appeared at No. 4, and captivated five perfons ; the particulars of this matter I cannot afcertain.

March 20, 1758. J. Morrifon, and J. Henry of Colrain, being near what is called north river, (a branch of Deerfield river), were fired on, and were both wounded ; capt. Morriffon's barn was burnt, and his cattle were killed the fame day.

March 21, 1759. The enemy again appeared at Colrain, and captivated Jofeph M'Ewers, with his wife. Mrs. M'Ewers, was killed by the enemy, after one day's travel, fhe being unable to proceed.

This is the laft account, which I can obtain, of mifchief done by the enemy, in the weftern frontiers, in the laft French war.

———— ————

APPREHENDING that it will not be difagreeable to the publick, I here fubjoin a circumftantial account of what is called the *fall fight*, which happened in May, 1676.

The following, I have taken in part, from Hubbard's hiftory of the Indian wars ; but principally from an atteſted copy of a manufcript, written by fome gentlemen who were in the action.

Several large bodies of Indians had affembled at different places about Deerfield. Two tribes had feated themfelves at the falls, one on the eaft, and the other on the weft fide

of

of the river. A little below the falls, upon an island, was another tribe. Another had placed themselves on the west side of the river, at a little distance above the falls : And a fifth had taken their residence at Cheapside.

These Indians, being previously informed, by some of their captives, that the forces were principally withdrawn from the neighbouring towns, had imprudently fallen into a state of unguarded security. The inhabitants being informed of this, by some prisoners, who had been so fortunate as to make their escape, determined to improve the opportunity, and if possible, extirpate them from this part of the country. All the soldiers, who could be raised, for this almost desperate expedition, both from the militia, and the standing forces, amounted to only one hundred and sixty. The standing forces were commanded by capt. Turner, of Boston. The volunteers by their own officers. Those from Springfield, by capt. Holyoke ; from Northampton, by ensign Lyman ; from Hadley, and Hatfield, by sergeants Kellogg, and Dickinson. The Rev. Hope Atherton, minister of the gospel, at Hatfield, a gentleman of publick spirit, accompanied the army. The pilots were messrs. Benjamin Wait, and Experience Hinsdale.

These troops marched from Hatfield May 17, 1676, a little before night. Passing Deerfield river, at Cheapside, they were heard by the Indian sentinel, who immediately alarmed the tribe, informing them, that horses had passed the river. Search was immediately made, at the usual fording place, which our troops had happily missed, having by mistake, crossed a little above, and the enemy finding no tracks, concluded, that their sentry had been deceived, and that what he heard, must have been the noise of moose, passing the river near the fording place. Meeting with no opposition from this tribe, our troops marched on, till they came to the falls. It was now about the break of day. According to their wishes, our army found the enemy in an unguarded situation, without even a sentinel. The reason why, at this time, they were thus surprisingly unguarded, was, the evening before they had been rioting upon milk, and roast beef, having been pillaging cows from the neighbouring towns. When the day opened, so that our army could distinguish friends from foes, they marched up and began the attack, by firing into the wigwams. The Indians awaking in surprise, and in their consternation sup-

L 2

posing

posing that they were attacked by their native enemies, cried, Mohawks! Mohawks! They soon, however, discovered their mistake; but being in no situation to make an immediate defence, great numbers were slain upon the spot, some, in their surprise, ran directly into the river, and were drowned; others betook themselves to their bark canoes, and having in their confusion forgot their paddles, were hurried down the falls, and dashed against the rocks; and many who had endeavoured to secrete themselves under the river banks, were discovered, and slain.

In this action the enemy, by their own confession, lost 300, women, and children included.

This victory, though great, and obtained with the loss of only one man, in the first onset, was yet, howeve, disastrous in the issue. The few who had not been slain, of this tribe, after recovering from their fright, and being joined by the neighbouring tribes, discovering the smallness of the number, by whom they had been thus furiously attacked, and by whom they had sustained such a loss, pursued, and harrassed the army on their retreat, with such fury, that thirty-seven were killed, and several were wounded.

This loss was imputed, in part, to the bodily infirmities of capt. Turner; and in part to the want of ammunition, which was the cause of an ill-timed and unguarded retreat.

A few, to the number of about twenty, did not quit the ground, with the main body of the army, but tarried behind, for the purpose of firing at some of the enemy who were crossing the river. These men soon found themselves under the necessity of disputing the ground, with a considerable body of the enemy, before they could recover their horses; but after a severe skirmish, obtained their object, and soon came up with the army, which was surrounded, and fought on their retreat for ten miles. Seven, or eight men, in the beginning of the retreat, were, by some accident, unfortunately separated from the army, and soon found themselves lost. The Indians afterwards gave the following account of them: That on Monday after the fight, eight Englishmen came to them, who were lost, and offered to surrender, on condition their lives might be spared; but, instead of giving them quarter, they took and burnt them in the following manner:—They first covered them with dry thatch, then set fire to it, and compelled them to run: When one covering was burnt off, they put

on

on another, and fo continued, till death delivered them from their hands.

This expedition was productive of very happy confequences, for the enemy were fo difconcerted in all their plans, and fo greatly difheartened, that they never after, during that war, gave any confiderable difturbance to the frontiers. From this expedition may be dated their decline in thefe parts.

In the above action was one Jonathan Wells, of Hatfield, then a youth in his 17th year, he was afterwards a gentleman improved in publick life, and fuftained a worthy character. The following is the fubftance of an attefted copy of the account, taken from his own mouth.

Mr. Wells was one of the 20 men abovementioned, who were under a neceffity of difputing the ground, for the purpofe of recovering their horfes. Soon after he had mounted, being in the rear, three of the enemy fired upon him ; one of their balls bruthed his hair, another wounded his horfe, and a third ftruck his thigh, in a place where it had before been broken with a cart wheel ; the ball did not wholly break his thigh anew, but fractured the end of one of the bones, which was a little projected over the other, it having been badly fet. Upon receiving the wound, it was with difficulty that Mr. Wells kept in his faddle. The Indians perceiving they had wounded him, preffed hard upon him. Mr. Wells, recovering a little from the firft fhock, and perceiving the enemy almoft upon him, prefented his gun, which gave them a check, and whilft they were charging, he made his efcape, and reached the company. He reprefented to capt. Turner, the danger to which the people in the rear were expofed, and urged him to return to their relief, or halt till they might come up ; but he anfwered, " It is better to lofe fome, than all." The army was now divided into feveral companies, one pilot crying, " If you will fave your lives, follow me ;" and another, " If you regard your fafety, follow me." Mr. Wells was now following a company, whofe courfe was towards a fwamp ; but perceiving that a body of the enemy were there, he left that company, who were all loft, and joined a fmall party, who were taking a different route ; but his horfe foon failing by reafon of his wound, and himfelf being much weakened by lofs of blood, he was left by this party, having only one, Jones, a wounded man to accompany him : They had no path to guide them, and

and were both unacquainted with the woods. They had
not travelled far, before Mr. Wells was separated from Jones,
and finding himself faint, eat a nutmeg which he had in his
pocket, upon which he revived. After having wandered
in the woods for some time, he came upon green river, and
he followed the course of it up, till he came to a place called the country farms; having passed the river he attempted to ascend a mountain on the west side, but fainted, and
fell from his horse. How long he lay in this condition he
knew not, but when he recovered, he found his horse
standing by him, and his bridle hanging on his hand. He
arose, tied his horse, and again laid himself down; but upon
reflection, finding himself already so weak as to be unable
to mount, concluded that he should have no farther use for
his horse, and being unwilling he should die at the tree, dis-
missed him; but unhappily forgot to take any provision
from his portmanteau, although it contained a plenty.
Towards night, being troubled with musquetoes, he struck
up a fire; but this almost proved his destruction; it arose,
and spread with such fury, among the leaves and trash, that
it was with difficulty, in his faint condition, he escaped
perishing in the flames. After he was out of danger, from
the fire, he again laid himself down to rest; but now new
fears arose; he imagined that the fire would direct the enemy where to find him; and serve to betray him into their
hands: Unwilling the enemy should be benefited by his
ammunition, he cast it to as great a distance as he could,
reserving only a charge or two for their use, should he fall
into their hands. After some time, finding his fire had
spread considerably, he took courage, put some tow into
his wounds, bound them up with his handkerchief, and
composed himself to sleep. In his sleep he dreamed, that
his grandfather came to him, and told him he was lost, and
must turn, and go down that river, till he should come to
the end of a mountain, where he would find a plain, upon
which he must travel, in order to find his way home.
When he awoke he found himself refreshed, his bleeding
stopped, and his strength recruited, and with the help of
his gun as a staff, he was able to walk, though but slowly.
The rising of the sun, convinced him, he was lost, and that
the course he intended to pursue was wrong. He had now
wandered six or seven miles farther from home, than when
he set out from the place of action. And though, at first,
he

he paid no attention to his dream, now he determined to follow the directions of it. Accordingly, he travelled down the river, found the end of the mountain, and soon came to the plain ; all of which, agreed to the representation in his dream.* Soon after he entered upon the plain, he found a foot path, which led him to the road, in which, the main body of the army returned. When he came to Deerfield river, he met with much difficulty in crossing ; the stream carrying his lame leg across the other, so that several of his first attempts were without effect. Finally, however, with the help of his gun, with much difficulty he reached the opposite shore. When he had ascended the bank, being greatly fatigued, he laid himself down under a walnut bush, and fell asleep. When he awoke, the first object that presented, was an Indian in a canoe, coming directly towards him. Mr. Wells now found himself in a very unhappy condition, being so disabled by his wounds that he could not flee, and his gun being so filled with gravel and sand, in crossing the river, that he could not fight. So soon however, as he perceived the Indian had discovered him, he presented his gun, which so affrighted him, that he leaped out of the canoe, leaving his own gun, and made his escape. Mr. Wells concluding that he would inform the whole tribe, who were only a few rods distant, went into a neighbouring swamp, and finding two logs lying near each other, and covered over with rubbish, he crept between them. He soon heard the noise of Indians ; but was not curious to look out after them. When the noise had ceased, he ventured to proceed forward. In Deerfield meadow he found some horses' bones, from which he scraped some matter, which served for food ; he also found two or three rotten beans, where the Indians had threshed, and also two blue-bird's eggs, which was all the sustenance he had till he reached home. He came to Deerfield town plat, on Saturday

* I doubt, whether, in this dream, there was any thing supernatural, as some may be ready to suppose. Mr. Wells, having wandered in the woods six or seven miles, must necessarily have had some doubts whether his course was right ; and his mind, when asleep, would more naturally employ itself on this subject, than any other ; because to find the way home, must have been his great object, when awake. His dreaming that his grandfather appeared to him, was nothing strange ; and his local situation at this time was such, that he could not be entirely unacquainted with the natural make of the ground ; and his thoughts running as they did, in this dream, would be natural ; the river was near him—the plain was before him—and the end of the mountain, near the side of the plain, if he had not previously seen it, would naturally be supposed.

day night about dark, but as there were no inhabitants present, the town having a little before been burnt, he continued his courfe in the evening.

He was often under great difcouragements, and frequently laid himfelf down to die, expecting to rife no more. He reached no farther than muddy brook as the fun rofe on Sabbath morning. Here, feeing a human head, which had been dug up by wild beafts. Mr. Wells, notwithftanding the diftreffes of his condition, ftopped to find the grave, which having found he laid the head to the body, and covered it with billets of wood, to defend it from the ravenous beafts of the wildernefs. After he had left the brook and entered upon the plain, he grew faint and very thirfty, but could obtain no water for a confiderable time ; he was, however, often refrefhed, by holding his face in the fmoke of burning knots of pine, which he frequently met with, as the woods were on fire. Mr. Wells arrived at Hatfield on the Sabbath, between meetings, and was received with inexpreffible joy, as one having arifen from the dead. He endured incredible pain, and diftrefs, with his wound, being confined feveral times to his bead, for fix months together ; and it was upwards of four years before he was found.

In this action was alfo the Rev. Mr. Atherton, minifter of the gofpel, in Hatfield. The following is the fubftance of a paragraph, which he delivered to his people the Sabbath after his return :

" In the hurry and confufion of the retreat, I was feparated from the army ; the night following, I wandered up and down among the dwelling places of the enemy, but none of them difcovered me. The next day, I tendered myfelf to them a prifoner, for no way of efcape appeared, and I had been a long time without food ; but notwithftanding I offered myfelf to them, yet, they accepted not the offer ; when I fpake they anfwered not ; and when I moved toward them they fled.* Finding they would not accept of me as a prifoner, I determined to take the courfe of the river and if poffible find the way home, and after feveral days of hunger, fatigue and danger, I reached Hatfield."

Deerfield, October 10th, 1793.

The

---

* There were various conjectures at the time, relative to this ftrange conduct of the Indians ; the moft probable one was, that it arofe from fome of their religious fuperftitions.

The following observations were added by Mr. T. PRINCE, *to the third edition, for the information of our younger people.*

THE reverend author of the preceeding history and sermon was a son of Mr. Samuel Williams, of Roxbury, where he was born Dec. 10, 1664; took his first degree at Harvard college in 1683; was ordained the first pastor of the church in Deerfield, in May, 1686.

And his first wife Eunice, murdered by the barbarous Indians, as before related, was the only daughter of the Rev. Mr. Eleazer Mather, first pastor of the church in Northampton, by his only wife, Mrs. Esther, the daughter of the reverend and famous Mr. John Warham, formerly a minister in Exeter, in England, who came to New-England in 1630, was the first teacher with the Rev. Mr. Maverick, pastor of the first church in Dorchester, near Boston; and in 1635, removed, with the greater part of his church, to Windsor, on Connecticut river, where he continued their pastor until he died. After the Rev. Mr. Eleazer Mather's death, his widow married the Rev. Mr. Solomon Stoddard, who succeeded him in the pastoral office at Northampton.

When Deerfield was destroyed, in February, 1703-4, it was in the first year of my living at Harvard college; and I well remember how generally and greatly affected were the good people of this province, with that terrible disaster.

His eldest son, Eleazer, being then in another town, escaped that calamity. The next commencement, by the encouragement and help of divers charitable people, especially in Boston, he entered Harvard college; and living in the chamber over me, I fell into an intimate acquaintance with him; and found him a person of eminent piety, humility, sincerity, and sweetness of temper, like his father. He took his first degree in 1708, and became the faithful pastor of the church in Mansfield in Connecticut, until he died.

His reverend father returning from captivity, and arriving at Boston, November 21, 1706, to the great joy of the people; and being informed that he was to preach the publick lecture there on December 6th, I, with many others, went down, and in an auditory exceedingly crowded and affected, I heard the sermon herewith reprinted. And in those times, there was such a tender union, affection, and christian simplicity, among the good people here, that, as
the

the apostle lively describes it, ' When one member of the
' society suffered, the whole body seemed to suffer with it ;
' and when one rejoiced, the whole rejoiced.'

By the like kind encouragement, the Rev. Mr. Williams
had his son Stephen Williams educated at Harvard college ;
who took his first degree in 1713 ; was ordained pastor of
a church in Springfield ; and is so extensively known and
valued, that his name only need to be mentioned ; as that of
his son Warham—who took his first degree in 1719, and
became the worthy pastor of the church in Waltham, formerly a part of Watertown ; not long since deceased.

The Rev. Mr. Williams, of Deerfield, used every May,
yearly, to come down to the general convention of the ministers of the province at Boston ; where he was always very
affectionately entertained.

At the convention in May, 1728, (being chosen the year
before) he preached a very moving sermon to the ministers ;
when I remember, he expressed his joy in the great advan-
tage we at that time had above the preceeding ministers, in
the general awakenings through the land, by the great
earthquake in October foregoing. And on June 12, 1729,
he died, greatly beloved and lamented.

And by the accounts above, we may learn, from the in-
stance of this one town only in our western frontiers of the
province of the Massachusetts bay, in New-England, what
horrible murders and desolations this province has suffered
from the French and Indians in all our wars with them ever
since the year 1675, when the Indians first broke out upon
us—and what numbers of the present people in Canada are
the children of this province, or descendants from them—
which, in case the sovereign God should ever lead a victorious
army of ours into Canada, will clearly justify us to all the
world, if we should bring every child and descendant of New-
England, yea of all the British colonies, away—especially
considering we should bring them into a much pleasanter
and more plenteous land and agreeable climate ; out of a
wretched land of darkness and slavery, both religious and
civil, into a land of glorious light and liberty. And may
the Almighty hasten it in his time !

                                             T. PRINCE.

Boston, Dec. 20, 1757.

                    F I N I S.